An hour upon the stage

An hour upon the stage

one-act plays
with study material
and dramatic activities

edited by
LAIRD ORR

McGraw-Hill Ryerson Limited
Toronto   Montreal

OOOOOOOOOOOOOOOOOOOOOOOOOOOOOOOO

An Hour upon the Stage

ISBN 0-07-077988-0

1 2 3 4 5 6 7 8 9 0   AP   0 9 8 7 6 5 4 3 2 1

Printed and bound in Canada

Canadian Cataloguing in Publication Data

Main entry under title:

An Hour upon the stage

For use in secondary schools.
ISBN 0-07-077988-0

1. One-act plays, Canadian (English).*   2. One-act plays, British.   3. One-act plays, American.
4. One-act plays—Study and teaching (Secondary).
I. Orr, Laird.

PN6120.O5H68   822'.041   C81-094537-1

OOOOOOOOOOOOOOOOOOOOOOOOOOOOOO
ACKNOWLEDGEMENTS

A Separate Peace, by Tom Stoppard. Reprinted by permission of Fraser & Dunlop Scripts Limited.

Trans-Canada Highway, by James Tallman. First published 1974 by Borealis Press, Ottawa, copyright © Borealis Press. This edition published by arrangement with Borealis Press.

The Boor, by Anton Chekov. Application for the right to perform or reproduce this play in any form must be made to Samuel French, Inc., 25 West 45th Street, New York, N.Y. 10036. Copies of this play, in individual paper covered acting editions, are available from Samuel French, Inc., 25 W. 45th St., New York, N.Y. 10036 or 7623 Sunset Blvd., Hollywood, Calif. 90046 or in Canada, Samuel French, (Canada Ltd.), 80 Richmond Street East, Toronto M5C 1P1, Canada.

Mother Figure, by Alan Ayckbourn from *Confusions*. Reprinted by permission of Margaret Ramsay Ltd., London, England.

Passacaglia, by Joan Mason Hurley from *Canadian One Act Plays for Women*, A Room of One's Own Press, 1975.

Augustus Does His Bit, by Bernard Shaw. Reprinted by permission of the Society of Authors on behalf of the Bernard Shaw estate.

Schubert's Last Serenade, by Julie Bovasso. Reprinted by permission of the author. All rights reserved, Samuel French (Canada) Limited, 80 Richmond Street East, Toronto, Ontario M5C 1P1. Professional royalty quoted on application to Samuel French (Canada) Limited.

○ ○ ○ ○ ○ ○ ○ ○ ○ ○ ○ ○ ○ ○ ○ ○

Contents

Foreword   *To the Teacher*

The plays:

OOOOOOOOOOOOOOOOOOOOOOOOOOOOOO
To the Teacher

The plays in this volume are predominantly contemporary works, and they have been selected to give the young high school student a chance to experience the theatre as it really is. While all the plays can be appreciated by young people, they have not been written with this audience in mind.

Drawn from the diverse Canadian, British, and American traditions, these plays reflect concerns which are both particular and universal.

Preceding each play are suggestions for activities to enhance the student's appreciation of the play before he or she reads it. These suggestions encompass improvisation, interviews, and research assignments.

The One-Act Play

One thing that makes a play different from a short story or a novel is the element of time. A novel can tell us about years in a person's life, a short story about weeks or days, but the action of a play (and especially a one-act play) may occupy only minutes. Those minutes must be carefully chosen by the playwright for they must be among the most important in the person's life.

Let's take an imaginary character named Steve. Steve has the most inflexible boss in the world. The novel and short story may tell us that Steve's anger has been building up for years. Finally, the boss pushes him too far and Steve decides he has to do something. But what? This is the moment that begins the play.

If the play is a good one, it will have conflict. Steve may have decided to somehow get rid of his boss; but there will be someone else, maybe the boss himself, who will do everything in his power to keep that from happening. You might think of this conflict as two boxers competing in a title fight. As the men struggle against each other, we the audience become more and more tense, waiting to see the outcome. This *struggle* is sometimes called the *rising action*. The events of the struggle make up the *plot*.

We like Steve and feel sorry for him, so we want him to win. The playwright can load the dice any way he or she likes, so let's say the outcome of the struggle (the climax) is that Steve succeeds in getting rid of his boss. After the climax, the struggle is past, but the play is not necessarily over. We will want to know if Steve will get away with the killing and, possibly, how he killed him. We call this last part of the play, coming after the *main* struggle is over, the *denouement*.

If a person has been convicted of murder, the execution will take place in the denouement. If Romeo and Juliet had been able to overcome their parents' objections, they would have been married in the denouement.

At the end of the play you should feel satisfied that the playwright has left no loose ends or unanswered questions. Generally, it is in the denouement that the playwright "wraps things up." If this hasn't been done, you'll know.

The setting of the play must be carefully chosen. Unlike television, the medium of playwrights doesn't allow them to jump around from place to place, at least not with a realistic set. A different setting makes the play slightly different. If the play were set in Steve's living room, we would learn more about the private Steve than if it were set in the office. In the office we would see him with his fellow workers; at home we would be more likely to see him with his family and friends.

Again, unlike what we see on television, the kind of action possible on a stage is limited. With the exception of a very few stage directions, a play seems only to be words when you read it on the page. But actors know that an audience needs to see movement if it is to remain interested. A play has as much action as a television program, but of a different variety. On television, action can come from the actors, from rapidly changing locations and from things like cars or helicopters. On the stage, all action must come from the actors and the actresses.

In less than an hour, a one-act play makes us feel as if we have known the character for years. When the character we are made to care about is happy, we are happy. When life turns against him or her, it turns against us. If we don't feel these emotions, the play has failed in its purpose.

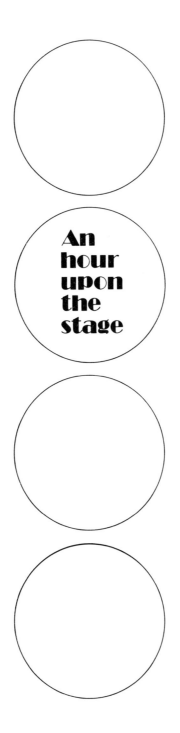

An
hour
upon
the
stage

A Separate Peace

by Tom Stoppard

Tom Stoppard is one of the most gifted playwrights working in the English language today. His plays always challenge the audience to look at the world in new ways. Among his many successful works are: *Rosencrantz and Guildenstern are Dead*, *The Real Inspector Hound*, and *Dirty Linen*. His most recent play, *Night and Day* opened in London, England in the fall of 1978. *A Separate Peace* was first published in 1969.

Before the Play

1. You have just announced to your parent or guardian that you have decided to quit school in order to have more time to do nothing. What would be the person's reaction? With a partner, improvise this conversation. Share your improvisation with a few of your classmates.

SCENE 1

The office of the Beechwood Nursing Home. Behind the reception counter sits a uniformed nurse. It is 2:30 a.m. A car pulls up outside. JOHN BROWN *enters. He is a biggish man in his late forties, with a well-lined face: calm, pleasant, implacable. He is wearing a nondescript suit and overcoat, and carrying two zipped grips. Looking around, he notes the neatness, the quiet, the flowers, the nice nurse, and is quietly pleased.*

BROWN   Very nice.
NURSE   Good evening . . .
BROWN   'Evening. A lovely night. Morning.
NURSE   Yes . . . Mr. . . . ?
BROWN   I'm sorry to be so late.
NURSE   (*Shuffling papers*) Were you expected earlier?
BROWN   No. I telephoned.
NURSE   Yes?
BROWN   Yes?
NURSE   I mean . . . ?
BROWN   You have a room for Mr. Brown.
NURSE   (*Realisation*) Oh! — Have you brought him?
BROWN   I brought myself. Knocked up a taxi by the station.
NURSE   (*Puzzled*) But surely . . . ?
BROWN   I telephoned, from the station.
NURSE   You said it was an emergency.
BROWN   That's right. Do you know what time it is?
NURSE   It's half past two.

2

BROWN   That's right. An emergency.
NURSE   (*Aggrieved*) I woke the house doctor.
BROWN   A kind thought. But it's all right. Do you want me to sign in?
NURSE   What is the nature of your emergency, Mr. Brown?
BROWN   I need a place to stay.
NURSE   Are you ill?
BROWN   No.
NURSE   But this is a private hospital . . .
BROWN   (*Smiles for the first time*) The best kind. What is a hospital without privacy? It's the privacy I'm after — that and the clean linen. . . . (*A thought strikes him*) I've got money.
NURSE   . . . the Beechwood Nursing Home.
BROWN   I require nursing. I need to be nursed for a bit. Yes. Where do I sign?
NURSE   I'm sorry, but admissions have to be arranged in advance except in the case of a genuine emergency — I have no authority—
BROWN   What do you want with authority? A nice girl like you. (*Moves*) Where have you put me?
NURSE   (*Moves with him*) And *you* have no authority—
BROWN   (*Halts*) That's true. That's one thing I've never had. (*He looks at her flatly*) I've come a long way.
NURSE   (*Wary*) Would you wait just a moment?
BROWN   (*Relaxes*) Certainly. Have you got a sign-in chit? Must abide by the regulations. Should I pay in advance?
NURSE   No, that's quite all right.
BROWN   I've got it — I've got it all here—

(*He starts trying to open one of the zipped cases, it jams and he hurts his finger. He recoils sharply and puts his finger in his mouth. The* DOCTOR *arrives, dishevelled from being roused*)

NURSE   Doctor — this is Mr. Brown.
DOCTOR   Good evening. What seems to be the trouble?
BROWN   Caught my finger.
DOCTOR   May I see? (BROWN *holds out his finger: the* DOCTOR *studies it, looks up: guardedly*) Have you come far?
BROWN   Yes. I've been travelling all day. (*The* DOCTOR *glances at the* NURSE) Not with my finger. I did that just now. Zip stuck.
DOCTOR   Oh. And what — er —

NURSE   Mr. Brown says there's nothing wrong with him.
BROWN   That's right — I —
NURSE   He just wants a bed.
BROWN   A room.
DOCTOR   But this isn't a hotel.
BROWN   Exactly.
DOCTOR   Exactly what?
BROWN   I don't follow you.
DOCTOR   Perhaps I'm confused. You see, I was asleep.
BROWN   It's all right. I understand. Well, if someone would show
   me to my room, I shan't disturb you any further.
DOCTOR   (*With a glance at the* NURSE) I don't believe we have any
   rooms free at the moment.
BROWN   Oh yes, this young lady arranged it.
NURSE   (*Self-defence*) He telephoned from the station. He said it
   was an emergency.
BROWN   I missed my connection.
DOCTOR   But you've come to the wrong place.
BROWN   No, this is the place all right. I don't want to be a nuisance.
DOCTOR   Did you try the pubs in the town?
BROWN   I'm not drunk.
DOCTOR   They have rooms.
BROWN   I've got a room. What's the matter?
DOCTOR   (*Pause*) Nothing — nothing's the matter. (*He nods at the
   nurse*) All right.
NURSE   Yes, doctor. (*Murmurs worriedly*) I'll have to make an entry
   . . .
DOCTOR   Observation.
BROWN   (*Cheerfully*) I'm not much to look at.
NURSE   Let me take those for you, Mr. Brown. (*The cases*)
BROWN   No, no, don't you. (*Picks up the cases*) There's nothing the
   matter with me. . . .

(BROWN *follows the* NURSE *inside. The* DOCTOR *watches them
   go, picks up* BROWN'S *form, and reads it. Then he picks
   up the phone and starts to dial*)

SCENE 2

BROWN'S *private ward. A pleasant room with a hospital bed
   and the usual furniture. One wall is almost all window*

4

and is curtained. BROWN *and the* NURSE *enter.* BROWN *puts his cases on the bed. He likes the room.*

BROWN   That's nice. I'll like it here.
NURSE   Will you be all right?
BROWN   Oh yes, I'm all right now. Picture window.
NURSE   The bathroom is across the corridor.
BROWN   (*Peering through curtains*) What's the view?
NURSE   Well, it's the drive and the gardens.
BROWN   Gardens. A front room. What could be nicer?
NURSE   (*Starts to open case*) Are your night things in here?
BROWN   Yes, I'll be very happy here.
NURSE   (*Opens the case, which is full of money — bank notes*) Oh — I'm sorry —
BROWN   (*He is not put out at all*) What time is breakfast?
NURSE   Eight o'clock.
BROWN   Lunch?
NURSE   Twelve o'clock.
BROWN   Tea?
NURSE   Three o'clock.
BROWN   Supper?
NURSE   Half past six.
BROWN   Cocoa?
NURSE   Nine.
BROWN   Matron's rounds twice a day?
NURSE   Yes.
BROWN   Temperatures?
NURSE   (*Turning back his bed*) Morning and evening.
BROWN   Change of sheets?
NURSE   Monday.
BROWN   Like clockwork. Lovely.
DOCTOR   (*Enters with* BROWN'S *form and Elastoplast*) Excuse me.
BROWN   I was just saying — everything's A1.
DOCTOR   I remembered your finger.
BROWN   I'd forgotten myself. It's nothing.
DOCTOR   Well, we'll just put this on overnight. (*He administers Elastoplast*)
BROWN   Must be wonderful to have the healing touch. I should get to bed now — you look tired.
DOCTOR   Thank you. I expect Matron will be along to discuss your case with you tomorrow.
BROWN   My finger?

DOCTOR   . . . Well, I expect she'd like to meet you.

BROWN   Be pleased to meet her.

DOCTOR   Yes . . . A final point, Mr. Brown. This form you filled in . . . Where it says permanent address, you've put down Beechwood Nursing Home.

BROWN   Yes. Well, you never know what the future brings, but for the while I like to think of it as home. . . .

SCENE 3

The hospital office. It is morning, and the DOCTOR *is at the desk, telephoning.*

DOCTOR   . . . I have absolutely no idea . . . The nurse said it looked like several hundred pounds. . . . His savings, yes. Frankly, I wouldn't be too keen on that — I don't really want the police turning up at the bedside of any patient who doesn't arrive with a life history. . . . I think we'd get more out of him than you would, given a little time, and we'd certainly keep you informed . . . No, he's not being difficult at all. . . . You don't need to worry about that — he doesn't seem very keen to run away. He seems quite happy. . . .

SCENE 4

BROWN'S *private ward.* BROWN *is in striped pajamas, eating off a tray. A second nurse — NURSE COATES (MAGGIE) — is waiting for him to finish so that she can take his tray away.* MAGGIE *is pretty and warm.*

BROWN   The point is not breakfast in bed, but breakfast in bed without guilt. Rich men's wives can bring it off, but if you're not a rich man's wife then you've got to be ill. Lunch in bed is more difficult, even for the rich. It's not any more expensive, but the disapproval is harder to ignore. To stay in bed for tea is almost impossible in decent society, and not to get up at all would probably bring in the authorities. Even if you had the strength of character there's probably a point where it becomes certifiable. But in a hospital it's not only understood — it's expected. That's the beauty of it. I'm not saying it's a great discovery — it's obvious really: but I'd say I'd got something.

MAGGIE   If you'd got something, there wouldn't be all this fuss.

BROWN   Is there a fuss? (MAGGIE *doesn't answer*) They should leave well alone. I'm paying my way. . . . Are you pretty full all the time?

MAGGIE   Not at the moment, not very.

BROWN   You'd think a place as nice as this would be very popular.

MAGGIE   Popular?

BROWN   I thought I might have to wait for a place, you know. Of course, it's a bit out the way, no passing trade, so to speak. I'm very fond of the English countryside myself.

MAGGIE   Where do you live?

BROWN   I've never lived. Only stayed.

MAGGIE   You should settle down somewhere.

BROWN   Yes, I've been promising myself this.

MAGGIE   Have you got a family?

BROWN   I expect so.

MAGGIE   Where are they?

BROWN   I lost touch.

MAGGIE   You should find them.

BROWN   (*Smiles*) Their name's Brown.

MATRON   (*Enters: she is not too old, and quite equable*) Good morning.

BROWN   Good morning to you. You must be matron.

MATRON   That's right.

BROWN   I must congratulate you on your hospital, it's a lovely place you run here. Everyone is so nice.

MATRON   Well, thank you, Mr. Brown. I'm glad you feel at home.

(*MAGGIE takes* BROWN'S *tray*)

BROWN   I never felt it there. Very good breakfast. Just what the doctor ordered. I hope he got a bit of a lie-in.

(*MAGGIE exits with the tray, closing the door*)

MATRON   Now, what's your problem, Mr. Brown?

BROWN   I have no problems.

MATRON   Your complaint.

BROWN   I have no complaints either. Full marks.

MATRON   Most people who come here have something the *matter* with them.

BROWN   That must give you a lot of extra work.

MATRON   But it's what we're here for. You see, you can't really stay unless there's something wrong with you.

BROWN   I can pay.

MATRON   That's not the point.

BROWN   What is the point?

MATRON   This is a hospital. What are you after?

BROWN   (*Sadly*) My approach is too straightforward. An ordinary malingerer or a genuine hypochondriac wouldn't have all this trouble. They'd be accepted on their own terms. All I get is a lot of personal questions. (*Hopefully*) Maybe I could *catch* something . . . But what difference would it make to you?

MATRON   We have to keep the beds free for people who need them.

BROWN   I need this room.

MATRON   I believe you, Mr. Brown — but wouldn't another room like this one do? — somewhere else? You see, we deal with physical matters — of the body —

BROWN   There's nothing wrong with my *mind*. You won't find my name on any list.

MATRON   I know.

BROWN   (*Teasing*) How do you know? (*She doesn't answer*) Go for the obvious, it's worth considering. I know what I like: a nice atmosphere — good food — clean rooms — a day and night service — no demands — cheerful staff— Well, it's *worth* thirty guineas a week. I won't be any trouble.

MATRON   Have you thought of going to a nice country hotel?

BROWN   Different kettle of fish altogether. I want to do nothing, and have nothing expected of me. That isn't possible out there. It worries them. They want to know what you're at — staying in your room all the time — they want to know what you're *doing*. But in a hospital it is understood that you're not doing anything, because everybody's in the same boat — it's the normal thing. Being a patient. That's what I'm cut out for, I think — I've got a vocation for it.

MATRON   But there's nothing wrong with you!

8

BROWN   That's why I'm *here*. If there was something wrong with me I could get into any old hospital — free. As it is, I'm quite happy to pay for *not* having anything wrong with me. If I catch something, perhaps I'll transfer. I don't know, though. I like it here. It depends on how my money lasts. I wouldn't like to go to a city hospital.

MATRON   But what do you want to do here?

BROWN   Nothing.

MATRON   You'll find that very boring.

BROWN   One must expect to be bored, in hospital.

MATRON   Have you been in hospital quite a lot?

BROWN   No. I've been saving up for it. . . . (*He smiles*)

SCENE 5

The hospital office. The DOCTOR *is phoning at a desk.*

DOCTOR   No luck? . . . Oh. Well, I don't know. The only plan we've got is to bore him out of here, but he's disturbingly self-sufficient. . . . Mmm, we've had a psychiatrist over . . . Well, he seemed amused . . . Both of them, actually; they were both amused . . . No, I shouldn't do that, he won't tell you anything. And there's one of our nurses — she's getting on very well with him . . . something's bound to come out soon . . .

SCENE 6

BROWN'S *ward.* BROWN *is in bed with a thermometer in his mouth.* MAGGIE *is taking his pulse. She removes the thermometer, scans it and shakes it.*

MAGGIE   I'm wasting my time here, you know.

BROWN   (*Disappointed*) Normal?

9

MAGGIE   You'll have to do better than that if you're going to stay.

BROWN   You're breaking my heart, Maggie.

MAGGIE   (*Almost lovingly*) Brownie, what are you going to do with yourself?

BROWN   Maggie, Maggie . . . Why do you want me to do something?

MAGGIE   They've all got theories about you, you know.

BROWN   Theories?

MAGGIE   Train-robber.

BROWN   That's a good one.

MAGGIE   A spy from the Ministry.

BROWN   Ho ho.

MAGGIE   Embezzler.

BROWN   Naturally.

MAGGIE   Eccentric millionaire.

BROWN   Wish I was. I'd have my own hospital, just for myself. I'd have the whole thing — with wards all named after dignitaries you've never heard of — and nurses, doctors, specialists, West Indian charladies, trolleys, rubber floors, sterilised aluminum, flowers, stretchers parked by the lifts, clean towels and fire regulations. . . . All built round me and staffed to feed me and check me and tick me off on a rota system.

MAGGIE   It's generally agreed you're on the run.

BROWN   No, I've stopped.

MAGGIE   Fixations have been mentioned.

BROWN   But you know better.

MAGGIE   I think you're just lazy.

BROWN   I knew you were the clever one.

MAGGIE   (*Troubled, soft*) Tell me what's the matter, Brownie?

BROWN   I would if there was.

MAGGIE   What do you want to stay here for then?

BROWN   I like you.

MAGGIE   You didn't know I was here.

BROWN   That's true. I came for the quiet and the routine. I came for the white calm, meals on trays and quiet efficiency, time passing and bringing nothing. That seemed enough. I never got it down to a person. But I like you — I like you very much.

MAGGIE   Well, I like you too, Brownie. But there's more in life than that.

MATRON   (*She enters*) Good morning.

BROWN   Good morning, matron.
MATRON   And how are we this morning?
BROWN   We're very well. How are you?
MATRON   (*Slightly taken aback*) I'm all right, thank you. Well, are you enjoying life?
BROWN   Yes thank you, matron.
MATRON   What have you been doing?
BROWN   Nothing.
MATRON   And what do you want to do?
BROWN   Nothing.
MATRON   Now really, Mr. Brown, this won't do, you know.
BROWN   Why not?
MATRON   You mustn't lose interest in life.
BROWN   I was never very interested in the first place.
MATRON   Wouldn't you like to get up for a while? Have a walk in the garden? There's no reason why you shouldn't.
BROWN   No, I suppose not. But I didn't come here for that. I must have walked thousands of miles, in my time.
MATRON   It's not healthy to stay in bed all day.
BROWN   Perhaps I'll *get* something.
MATRON   Well, isn't there anything you could do indoors?
BROWN   What do the other patients do?
MATRON   The other patients are here because they are not well.
BROWN   I thought patients did things . . . (*Vaguely*) Raffia-work . . .
MATRON   Does that appeal to you?
BROWN   No.
MATRON   I suppose you wouldn't like to make paper flowers?
BROWN   What on earth for? You've got lots of real ones.
MATRON   *You* haven't got any.
BROWN   Well, no one knows I'm here.
MATRON   Then you must tell somebody.
BROWN   I don't want them to know.
MATRON   Who?
BROWN   Everybody.
MATRON   You'll soon get tired of sitting in bed.
BROWN   Then I'll sit by the window. I'm easily pleased.
MATRON   I can't let you just languish away in here. You must do *something*.
BROWN   (*Sighs*) All right. What?
MATRON   We've got basket-weaving . . .?
BROWN   Then I'll be left alone, will I?

SCENE 7

The hospital office. The DOCTOR *is on the phone.*

DOCTOR   Well, *I* don't know — how many John Browns *are* there in Somerset House? . . . Good grief! . . . Of course, if it's any consolation it may not be his real name . . . I know it doesn't help . . . That's an idea, yes . . . His fingerprints . . . No, no, I'll get them on a glass or something — Well, he might have been in trouble some time. . . .

SCENE 8

BROWN'S *ward.* BROWN *is working on a shapeless piece of basketry.* MATRON *enters.*

MATRON   What is it?
BROWN   Basketwork.
MATRON   But what is it for?
BROWN   Therapy.
MATRON   You're making fun of me.
BROWN   It is functional on one level only. If that. *You'd* like me to make a sort of laundry basket and lower myself in it out of the window. That would be functional on *two* levels. At least. (*Regards the mess sadly*) And I'm not even blind. Ladies and gentlemen — a failure! Now I suppose you'll start asking me questions again.
MATRON   (*Silently dispossesses* BROWN *of his basketry*) What about *painting,* Mr. Brown?
BROWN   (*That strikes a chord*) Painting . . . I used to do a bit of painting.
MATRON   Splendid. Would you do some for me?
BROWN   Paint in here?
MATRON   Nurse Coates will bring you materials.
BROWN   What colours do you like?

MATRON   I like all colours. Just paint what you fancy. Paint scenes
from your own life.
BROWN   Clever! Should I paint my last place of employment?
MATRON   I'm trying to help you.
BROWN   I'm sorry. I know you are. But I don't need help.
Everything's fine for me. (*Pause*) Would you like me to paint
English countryside?
MATRON   Yes, that would be nice.

SCENE 9

The hospital office. The DOCTOR *is on the phone.*

DOCTOR   No . . . well, we haven't got anything against him really.
He's not doing any *harm*. No, he pays regularly. We can't
really refuse. . . . He's got lots left . . .

SCENE 10

BROWN'S *ward.* BROWN *is painting English countryside all
over one wall. He hasn't got very far but one sees the
beginnings of a simple pastoral panorama, competent
but amateurish.* MAGGIE *enters, carrying cut flowers in
a vase.*

MAGGIE   Hello — (*She notices*)
BROWN   I'll need some more paint.
MAGGIE   (*Horrified*) Brownie! I gave you drawing paper!
BROWN   I like space. I like the big sweep — the contours of hills all
flowing — I don't paint leaves, I make you see trees in
clumps of green.
MAGGIE   Matron will have a fit.
BROWN   What are the flowers?
MAGGIE   You don't deserve them.

BROWN   Who are they from?

MAGGIE   Me.

BROWN   Maggie!

MAGGIE   I didn't buy them.

BROWN   Pinched them?

MAGGIE   Picked them.

BROWN   A lovely thought. Put them over there. I should bring *you* flowers.

MAGGIE   I'm not ill.

BROWN   Nor am I. Do you like it?

MAGGIE   Very pretty.

BROWN   I'm only doing it to please matron really. I could do with a bigger brush. There's more paint, is there? I'll need a lot of blue. It's going to be summer in here.

MAGGIE   It's summer outside. Isn't that good enough for you?

BROWN   (*Stares out of the window: gardens, flowers, trees, hills*) I couldn't stay out there. You don't get the benefits.

MAGGIE   (*Leaving*) I'll have to tell matron, you know.

BROWN   You don't get the looking after. And the privacy. (*He considers*) I'll have to take the curtains down.

SCENE 11

The hospital office.

MATRON   It's not as if he was psychotic.

DOCTOR   Or Picasso.

MATRON   What did the psychiatrist think?

DOCTOR   He likes it.

MATRON   About *him*.

DOCTOR   He likes him too.

MATRON   (*Sour*) He's likeable.

DOCTOR   He knows what he's doing.

MATRON   Hiding.

DOCTOR   From what? . . . (*Thoughtfully*) I just thought I'd let him stay the night. I wanted to go back to bed and it seemed the easiest thing to do. I thought that in the morning . . . Well, I'm not sure what I thought would happen in the morning.

MATRON   He's not simple — he's giving nothing away. Not even to Nurse Coates.

14

DOCTOR Well, keep her at it.
MATRON She doesn't need much keeping.

SCENE 12

BROWN'S *ward*. BROWN *has painted a whole wall and is working on a second one.* MAGGIE *sits on the bed.*

MAGGIE That was when I started nursing, after that.
BROWN Funny. I would have thought your childhood was all to do with ponies and big stone-floored kitchens . . .
MAGGIE Goes to show. What was your childhood like?
BROWN Young . . . I wish I had more money.
MAGGIE You've got a lot. You must have had a good job . . .?
BROWN Centre-forward for Arsenal.
MAGGIE You're not fair! You don't give me anything in return.
BROWN This painting's for you, Maggie . . . If I'd got four times as much money, I'd take four rooms and paint one for each season. But I've only got money for the summer.
MAGGIE What will you do when it's gone?
BROWN (*Seriously*) I don't know. Perhaps I'll get ill and have to go to hospital. But I'll miss you, Maggie.
MAGGIE If you had someone to look after you you wouldn't have this trouble.
BROWN What trouble?
MAGGIE If you had someone to cook your meals and do your laundry you'd be all right, wouldn't you?
BROWN It's the things that go with it.
MAGGIE You should have got married. I bet you had chances.
BROWN Perhaps.
MAGGIE It's not too late.
BROWN You don't think so?
MAGGIE You're attractive.
BROWN (*Pause*) What are you like when you're not wearing your uniform?
MAGGIE (*Saucy*) Mr. Brown!
BROWN (*Innocent, angry*) I didn't mean —!
MAGGIE (*Regretful*) Oh, I'm sorry. . . .

15

BROWN   (*Calm*) I can't think of you not being a nurse. It belongs to
another world I'm not part of any more.

MAGGIE   What have you got about hospitals?

BROWN   A hospital is a very dependable place. Anything could be
going on outside. Since I've been in here — there could be a
war on, and for once it's got nothing to do with me. I don't
even know about it. Fire, flood and misery of all kinds,
across the world or over the hill, it can all go on, but this is a
private ward; I'm paying for it. (*Pause*) There's one thing
that's always impressed me about hospitals — they've all
got their own generators. In case of power cuts. And water
tanks. I mean, a hospital can carry on, set loose from the
world. The meals come in on trays, on the dot — the dust
never settles before it's wiped — clean laundry at the
appointed time — the matron does her round and
temperatures are taken; pulses too, taken in pure conditions,
not affected by anything outside. You need never know
anything, it doesn't touch you.

MAGGIE   That's not true, Brownie.

BROWN   I know it's not.

MAGGIE   Then you shouldn't try and make it true.

BROWN   I know I shouldn't.

(Pause)

MAGGIE   It that all there is to it, then?

BROWN   You've still got theories?

MAGGIE   There's a new one. You're a retired forger.

BROWN   Ha! The money's real enough.

MAGGIE   I know.

BROWN   How do you know?

MAGGIE   (*Shamefaced*) They had it checked.

BROWN   (*Laughs*) They've got to make it difficult. I've got to be a
crook or a lunatic.

MAGGIE   Then why don't you tell them where you came from?

BROWN   They want to pass me on. But they don't know who to, or
where. I'm happy here.

MAGGIE   Haven't you been happy anywhere else?

BROWN   Yes. I had a good four years of it once.

MAGGIE   In hospital?

BROWN   No, that was abroad.

MAGGIE   Where have you been?

BROWN   All over. I've been among French, Germans, Greeks, Turks, Arabs. . . .

MAGGIE   What were you doing?

BROWN   Different things in different places. (*Smiles*) I was painting in France.

MAGGIE   An artist?

BROWN   Oh very. Green and brown. I could turn a row of tanks into a leafy hedgerow. Not literally. Worse luck.

SCENE 13

The hospital office. The DOCTOR *is on the phone.*

DOCTOR   . . . He meant camouflage . . . Well, I realise that, but there are a number of points to narrow the field . . . His age, for one thing. I *know* they were all the same age . . . Must be records of some kind . . . Service in France and Germany, probably Cyprus, Middle East — Aden possibly . . .

SCENE 14

BROWN'S *ward.* BROWN *has painted two walls and is working on a third.*

MAGGIE   It's very nice, Brownie. Perhaps you'll be famous and people will come here to see your mural.

BROWN   I wouldn't let them in.

MAGGIE   After you're dead. In a hundred years.

BROWN   Yes, they could come in then.

MAGGIE   What will you do when you've finished the room?

BROWN   Go back to bed and pick up the threads of my old life. It'll be nice in here. Hospital routine in a pastoral setting. That's kind of perfection, really.

MAGGIE   You could have put your bed in the garden.

BROWN   What's the date?

MAGGIE   The 27th.
BROWN   I've lasted well, haven't I?
MAGGIE   How old are you?
BROWN   Twice your age.
MAGGIE   Forty-four?
BROWN   And more (*Looking close*) What are you thinking?
MAGGIE   Only thinking.
BROWN   Yes?
MAGGIE   Before I was born, you were in the war.
BROWN   (*Moves*) Yes. Private Brown.
MAGGIE   Was it awful being in the war?
BROWN   I didn't like the first bit. But in the end it was very nice.
MAGGIE   What happened to you?
BROWN   I got taken prisoner.
MAGGIE   Oh. Well, you're still private, aren't you, Brownie?
BROWN   Better than being dead.
MAGGIE   Being private?
BROWN   A prisoner. . . . Four years.
MAGGIE   Is that where you were happy?
BROWN   Yes. . . . Funny thing, that camp. Up to then it was all terrible. Chaos — all the pins must have fallen off the map. The queue on the beach — dive bombers and bullets. Oh dear, yes. The camp was like breathing out for the first time in months. I couldn't believe it. It was like winning, being captured. Well, it gets different people in different ways. Some couldn't stand it and some went by the book — yes, it's a duty to escape. They were digging like ferrets. They had a hole out of my hut right into the pines. There were twenty in the hut and I watched all nineteen of them go off. They were all back in a week except one who was dead. I didn't care what they called me, I'd won. The war was still going on but I wasn't going to it any more. They gave us food, life was regulated, in a box of earth and wire and sky, and sometimes you'd hear an aeroplane miles up, but it couldn't touch you. On my second day I knew what it reminded me of.
MAGGIE   What?
BROWN   Here. It reminded me of here.

SCENE 15

The hospital office. Present are the DOCTOR, MATRON *and* MAGGIE. *The* DOCTOR *is holding a big book — a ledger of admissions, his finger on a line.*

DOCTOR   John Brown. And an address. (*Looks up.*) It was obvious. (*To* MAGGIE) Well done.
MAGGIE   (*Troubled*) But does it make any difference?
MATRON   What was he doing round here?
DOCTOR   Staying with relatives — or holiday, we can find out.
MATRON   So long ago?
DOCTOR   Compound fracture — car accident. The driver paid for him . . . Well, something to go on at last!
MAGGIE   But he hasn't done anything wrong, has he?

SCENE 16

BROWN'S *ward. The painting nearly covers the walls.* BROWN *is finishing it off in one corner.*

BROWN   I was a Regular, you see, and peace didn't match up to the war I'd had. There was too much going on.
MAGGIE   So what did you do then?
BROWN   This and that. Didn't fancy a lot. I thought I'd like to be a lighthouse keeper but it didn't work out. Didn't like the company.
MAGGIE   Company?
BROWN   There were three of us.
MAGGIE   Oh.
BROWN   Then I thought I'd be a sort of monk, but they wouldn't have me because I didn't believe, didn't believe enough for their purposes. I asked them to let me stay without being a proper monk but they weren't having any of that. . . . What I need is a sort of monastery for agnostics.
MAGGIE   Like a hospital for the healthy.
BROWN   That's it.

MAGGIE   (*Exasperated*) Brownie!
BROWN   (*He paints*) Shouldn't you be working, or something?
MAGGIE   I'll go if you like.
BROWN   I like you being here. Just wondered.
MAGGIE   Wondered what?
BROWN   I'm telling you about myself, aren't I? I shouldn't put you in that position — if they find out they'll blame you for not passing it on.
MAGGIE   But you haven't done anything wrong, have you, Brownie?
BROWN   Is that what you're here for?
MAGGIE   No.
BROWN   (*Finishes off the painting and stands back*) There.
MAGGIE   It's lovely.
BROWN   Yes. Quite good. It'll be nice, to sit here inside my painting. I'll enjoy that.

SCENE 17

The hospital office. The DOCTOR *is on the phone.*

DOCTOR   . . . Brown. John Brown — yes, he was here before, a long time ago — we've got him in the records — Mmm — and an address. We'll start checking . . . there must be *somebody*. . . .

SCENE 18

BROWN'S *ward. The walls are covered with paintings.* BROWN *is sitting on the bed. The door opens and a strange nurse —* NURSE JONES *— enters with* BROWN'S *lunch on a tray.*
JONES   Are you ready for lunch —? (*Sees the painting*) My, my, aren't you clever — it's better than anyone would have thought.
BROWN   Where's Maggie?
JONES   Nurse Coates? I don't know.

BROWN   But — she's my nurse.
JONES   Yours? Well, she's everybody's.
BROWN   (*Worried*) You don't understand — she's looking after *me*, you see.

(*The* DOCTOR *enters;* NURSE JONES *leaves*)

DOCTOR   (*Cheerful*) Well, Mr. Brown — good news!
BROWN   (*Wary*) Yes?
DOCTOR   You're going to have visitors.
BROWN   Visitors?
DOCTOR   Your sister Mabel and her husband. They were amazed to hear from you.
BROWN   They didn't hear from *me*.
DOCTOR   They're travelling up tomorrow. All your friends had been wondering where you'd got to —
BROWN   (*Getting more peevish*) What friends?
DOCTOR   Well, there's an old army friend, isn't there — what's his name —?
BROWN   I don't know. Where's Nurse Coates gone?
DOCTOR   Nowhere. She's round about. I think she's on nights downstairs this week. I understand that you were here once before — as a child.
BROWN   Yes.
DOCTOR   You *are* a dark horse, aren't you? To tell you quite frankly, we did wonder about you — some quite romantic ideas, not entirely creditable either —
BROWN   I told you — I told you there was nothing like that — Why couldn't you —?
DOCTOR   Your brother-in-law said something about a job, thought you might be interested.
BROWN   (*Angrily*) You couldn't leave well alone, could you?
DOCTOR   (*Pause; not phoney any more*) It's not enough, Mr. Brown. You've got to . . . *connect*. . . .

SCENE 19

The hospital office. BROWN *appears, dressed, carrying his bags, from the direction of his room. He sees* MAGGIE *and stops. She sees him.*

MAGGIE   Brownie! Where are you going?

BROWN   Back.

MAGGIE   Back where? (*He does not answer*) You've got nothing to run for, have you. Nothing to hide. I *know* you haven't.

BROWN   I know you know. They've been busy . . . I wasn't worth the trouble, you know.

MAGGIE   You blame me.

BROWN   No. No. I don't, *really*. You had to tell them, didn't you?

MAGGIE   I'm sorry — I —

BROWN   You thought it was for the best.

MAGGIE   Yes, I did. I still do. It's not good for you, what you're doing.

BROWN   How do you know? — *you* mean it wouldn't be good for *you*. How do you know what's good for me?

MAGGIE   They're coming tomorrow. Family, friends; isn't that good?

BROWN   I could have found them, if I'd wanted. I didn't come here for that. (*Comes up to her*) They won. (*Looks out through front doors*) I feel I should breathe in before going out there.

MAGGIE   I can't let you go, Brownie.

BROWN   (*Gently mocking.*) Regulations?

MAGGIE   I can't.

BROWN   I'm free to come and go. I'm paying.

MAGGIE   I know — but it *is* a hospital.

BROWN   (*Smiles briefly*) I'm not ill. Don't wake the doctor, he doesn't like being woken. (*Moves*) Don't be sorry — I had a good time here with you. Do you think they'll leave my painting?

MAGGIE   Brownie . . .

BROWN   Trouble is, I've always been so *well*. If I'd been *sick* I would have been all right. (*He goes out into the night*)

THE END

After the Play Suggestions:

For Writing and Discussion

1. John Brown wants to do only one thing in life: nothing. Because

he isn't sick, the hospital authorities eventually force him to leave. Why, in your opinion, does Brown upset them so much?

2. Imagine that you're sick of working, and that you have decided to "retire" to your bedroom for a two or three-week rest. Your family has agreed to bring you your meals and anything else you might need. Apart from food, describe the things that you would want to have with you.

3. Brown seems to be quite content doing absolutely nothing, until he is pressured by the staff. The stage design of his room at the nursing home must make clear that there is no form of entertainment available to him. Describe how you would demonstrate this fact in a set design. Accompany your description with a drawing or diagram.

4. a) In the introduction to this book, a play is described as a struggle between boxers. If Brown is one boxer, who is (are) the other(s)?
   b) What is the struggle about?
   c) What event in the play shows that the main struggle is over? (In other words, what is the climax of the play?)
   d) What happens after the climax (in the denouement)?

5. Is Brown crazy? Explain your answer carefully.

6. Why can't Maggie help Brown?

7. Is it possible to do nothing and have a successful life? Discuss this in detail.

For Presentation

Divide the class into small groups of two or three. Assign each group a section of the script so that everyone has something to do. Spend some time with your group practising the scene out loud. Recall the improvisation that you did before reading the play. Think how this can help you understand the characters' feelings. When everyone is ready, set up three or four chairs at the front of the room or arrange your desks so that each person in the class can see one another. Now have all the groups read through their sections in order.

Hints:

Assume that the class is hard-of-hearing. Try not to look at the page any more than you have to. Speak the lines as though you can see the person you are talking to in a mirror at the back of the room.

Trans-Canada Highway

by James Tallman

James Tallman, a resident of Kelowna, British Columbia, is a television copywriter in Vancouver.

Before the Play

Talk to someone who has hitchhiked a long distance. Get this person to tell you their best hitchhiking story. Tell it to the class *as though it is your own story.*

CHARACTERS:

SLIM   *A young man about 21 or 22, slightly long-haired. He wears blue jeans, Levis cowboy shirt, tan desert boots. He is used to the road dust between his teeth.*

JANE   *A young woman about 18 or 19. She wears an unzipped wind-breaker over a white T-shirt, cord pants, tennis shoes. Reasonably sure of herself, but leaving home for the first time.*

Author's Note: *The direction of "Looking down the road" is looking towards the audience.*

SCENE

(A road sign that says "Speed Limit 60" stands in the middle of the stage. Clumps of grass grow about its base. The stage is low-lit except the area around the sign. SLIM *sits beneath the sign, leaning his back up against the side of the post. A sleeping bag is rolled up and lies against the side of the post. A wind-breaker is draped carelessly across the sleeping bag. A car is heard approaching at high speed.* SLIM *lifts his right arm, holding his thumb out. The car is heard roaring past.* SLIM *lets his arm down, looks up the road behind him where the car has gone.* Slim *sighs. He stands up, stretches his legs. He groans, sits down, takes off the shoe and sock of one foot, looks at the sole of his foot)*

SLIM Wow.

*(*SLIM *feels his foot tenderly. He is inspecting it when another car roars by. He holds up his right thumb but does not look up, choosing instead to concentrate on his foot. The car does not stop.* SLIM *puts his sock and shoe back on. He stands up and looks down the road. As he does,* JANE *enters from upper stage right. She has a bulging pack sack on her back that includes a sleeping bag lashed on.* SLIM *hears her and turns)*

SLIM Howdy.
JANE H'lo.
SLIM Where'd you come from?
JANE Back there *(Nods head)* . . . I'm hitch-hiking.
SLIM *(As if to say, "I never would have guessed")* Really?

(Another car approaches. SLIM *holds out his thumb.* JANE *watches him, but does not hold her thumb out. The car passes)*

SLIM *(Watching car disappear)* Hmm . . .

*(*JANE *lets her pack down)*

JANE Cooling off a little, isn't it?
SLIM *(Staring down road)* Yep . . . *(Looks at her closely for first time)* Hitching, hey? You been on the road very long?
JANE No . . . I'm just starting out . . . *this* trip. Farmer let me off by that side road back a ways . . . You been here long?
SLIM A while. In fact, I been walking most of the day. Guess it's true what they say — a girl hitch-hikes, a guy hikes.
JANE Yeah . . . Where are you going?
SLIM Oh, down the road.
JANE Where you from?
SLIM Here and there.
JANE Do you always talk like that?

27

SLIM   Only when I want to be cool.

JANE   Don't you have any special place to go?

SLIM   I don't know.

JANE   What do you mean?

SLIM   Well . . . I'm looking for home, and I haven't found it yet . . . I got itchy feet, except when I got sore feet.

JANE   Don't you have a home at all?

SLIM   Well, I got a *house*, if that's what you mean . . . I lived in it for a long time, but the whole time I kept feeling I shoulda been living somewhere else. Do you know what I mean?

JANE   No, I've always lived around here.

SLIM   Ah, well, then, you shouldn't be expected to know what I mean. You *know* where your home is. Right here.

JANE   But I feel restless, too, just like you. I got itchy feet, too.

SLIM   Yeah, but it's not the same.

JANE   (*Defensively*) Whatta ya' mean not the same? I can travel around just as well as you can. I've got a thumb, too! (*Holds her thumb up*)

SLIM   Yeah, I can see.

JANE   And I don't know where I'm going, either.

SLIM   Oh, dear. Yet another mixed-up child.

(A car goes past. SLIM *holds up a thumb briefly)*

JANE   (*Haughtily*) I'm not mixed-up and I'm not a child!

SLIM   But you're poor?

JANE   No. — Yes!

SLIM   Only when you want to be, you mean.

JANE   Everything I need is in my pack! (*Slim looks at her bulging pack*) I travel light when I want to.

SLIM   Light? I'd sure hate to have to *walk* very far with all that.

JANE   I can take care of myself.

SLIM   I'm glad of that. I have enough to think about just taking care of *myself*.

JANE   Look, if I annoy you so much, as you seem to be making it so obvious that I am, why don't you just head off down the road?

*(*SLIM *looks at her as if he can't quite believe what he's hearing)*

SLIM   (*Patiently*) Ah, you may have noticed — *I* was here first. That means *you* head off down the road. I don't really feel like company today anyway. My feet hurt.

JANE   I'm so touched.

SLIM   Yeah. I can tell.

JANE   *I* just walked two miles down the road myself.

SLIM   You mean you've been driven away once already today? Maybe you should just go back home.

JANE   (*With a hint of suspicion*) Where you from, anyway?

SLIM   Well, lessee . . . (*Sits down, leans against sign post*) Last night, I slept in a field. I didn't get there 'til after dark. Thought it was a hay field — you know, a field for growing grain. I woke up at dawn. There was the hugest black bull you ever saw standing about twelve feet off. Did I ever clear out of *there* fast! Didn't even get out of my sleeping bag. Just rolled over about four times until I'd rolled under the fence. . . . (*Baiting her*) You know . . . I haven't had a bath in four days.

JANE   Only that long, was it?

SLIM   Wait till *you've* been on the road for a couple of days, and you get road dust and car fumes in your hair and under your toe nails and everywhere else. 'Bout as much fun as spending the rest of your life under this sign.

JANE   You could always stop somewhere for a bath, couldn't you?

SLIM   Say, ah, do you know what you're getting yourself into, kid? How much hitching have you actually done?

JANE   I told you — I'm not a child. I'm not a kid, either.

SLIM   (*Grunts impatiently*) Yeah, okay . . . But how much have you done?

JANE   A lot . . . (*Wilting under his gaze*) Well, quite a lot.

SLIM   From the farm to the post office, you mean?

JANE   No! . . . I mean, lots farther than that.

SLIM   Yeah?

JANE   Yes. Don't you believe me?

SLIM   No.

JANE   Well, I have.

SLIM   Okay, you have . . . You got a raincoat in that pack?

JANE   (*Proudly*) Yes.

SLIM   Good, because I think it's going to rain.

JANE   You do? (*Glances at sky*) How would you know?

SLIM   My vast experience.

JANE   (*Snorts derisively*) Well, that's fine with me. I like the rain. And it means I can *use* my raincoat . . . Do you have one?

SLIM   No.

JANE   You don't? Huh! I thought you knew your way around. Or are you just so tough you don't need it? It could mean a free bath.

SLIM   I'm splitting a gut laughing.

JANE   I noticed.

SLIM   Good.

JANE   I don't think I like you very much.

(SLIM *laughs sardonically as a car goes past. He holds out his thumb. The car keeps going*)

JANE   What's so funny?

SLIM   What makes you so sure I like you?

JANE   (*Tentatively*) . . . Don't you?

SLIM   I don't know. You keep putting me down.

JANE   I don't put *you* down. You keep putting *me* down! . . . How have I put you down?

SLIM   Well, you tell me to take a bath . . . That's not very nice . . . (*Shakes his head*) You know, when you're getting a free ride, you ride as far as you can. You don't say, "All right, driver, I'll just stop now for my shower and shave and then we'll continue when I'm good and ready."

JANE   I know *that*.

SLIM   Yeah? You know, I once knew a guy who was hitching through the mountains, and you know what?

(JANE *stands at the road's edge, staring down the road*)

JANE   (*Feigning disinterest*) What?

SLIM   They get half way through a pass, right in the middle of it, about 30 miles each way to the nearest gas station — not even town — just the nearest gas station, and the guy stopped and said, "Okay, get out."

JANE   (*Facing* SLIM) Get out?

SLIM   Yep. And so he did, because what can you do? The guy drove off, just like that, left him right there in the middle of the night, and you never get a ride at night, especially in a place like that, and it had just stopped raining, so he had to walk because it was too wet to roll out his sleeping bag.

JANE   (*Nervously*) What happened to him?

SLIM   Oh, nothing much. He got a ride the next morning that took him all the way to where he was going.

JANE   Does that happen very often?

SLIM   Getting rides to where you're going?

JANE   No, I mean being left off in the middle of nowhere.

SLIM   Oh, once in a while.

JANE   Has it ever happened to you?

SLIM   No, not like that, at least. You never can tell with some guys, though. You talk when they don't want to, they think you're being over-friendly, and they find some excuse to let you off at the next town. (JANE *looks back down the road*) Or, if you don't want to talk when they do, they think you're subversive and when you're sitting in the can at the next gas station, you suddenly hear their car roar off down the highway.

JANE   Oh.

SLIM   You just can't tell what it is with some guys. What you've done.

(JANE *sits by her pack.* SLIM *looks at her. He decides he has put her in her place and takes pity on her*)

SLIM   Don't worry about it, though. Most of the time you get rides from people who have been through this themselves and know what it's like, or sometimes they take pity on you, which is okay, because not many do, or sometimes they're just curious and want to find out what you're like.

(*They sit silently watching down the road. A car is heard approaching far off in the distance*)

SLIM   Here comes another . . . Wonder if he'll stop? (SLIM *gets to his feet*) . . . (*looks hard down the road*) Ah . . . Volkswagen! (*Puts his thumb out*) Come on, guy, stop.

JANE   (*Gets to her feet*) Do you think he will?

(JANE *stand behind* SLIM *and watches how he holds his thumb out. She copies him uncertainly*)

31

SLIM   Maybe. One out of three Volkswagens stop, you know.

(They watch expectantly. As the roar increases, SLIM starts speaking and is finally drowned out as the car zooms by and he sees it is not going to stop)

SLIM   Slow down, guy . . . Stop. Pick us up, guy, pick us up! . . . What'sa matter with you, guy? ! . . .

(SLIM spins around and watches the car disappear. He still holds his thumb in the air, slowly lets it down)

SLIM   Hmm. Maybe it was one out of four.
JANE   I see another car coming.
SLIM   *(Facing down the road again)* Yeah . . . Looks like a Rambler. They stop a lot.
JANE   Do you think he will?
SLIM   Don't know . . . *(Suddenly notices JANE is standing behind him)* — Here, look, whatta' you doing *behind* me? You gotta be out in front. Chick's always gotta be out in front.

(JANE moves hesitantly out in front of SLIM. She hopes she is holding her thumb in an experienced way)

JANE   *(Hopeful)* Is he stopping?
SLIM   . . . Naw . . . He's just checking us out.

(Car roars past)

SLIM   . . . *(Matter of factly)* There he goes. *(Drops his arm to his side)* Gees, my feet are sore!

(SLIM sits down again, leaning against the sign post. JANE remains standing, paces up and down once or twice, stops to look down the road)

SLIM   Anything?

JANE   No —. . .

SLIM   (*Sighs, chomps on piece of grass*) Hmm. Kind of slow today, I guess.

JANE   (*Doubtfully*) What's the *longest* you've ever stayed in one place?

SLIM   Hitching?

JANE   Yes.

SLIM   Oh . . . Once I was in a place for four days. Can't remember the name of the place . . . I'll never forget where it is, though. I'm *never* getting off there again.

JANE   Four days? (*Her voice almost breaks*) Where was it?

SLIM   Place like this, actually.

JANE   A place like this? (*She sits by her pack again*)

SLIM   Yeah . . . (*He looks at her*) But don't worry. I was with two other guys. Now there's just you and me. It's always easier for a guy and a chick to get a ride. Easiest of all, in fact.

JANE   Is it?

SLIM   Sure. People don't feel so threatened by a girl and a guy hitching together. Not like they do when they see three guys on the side of the road. You know what I mean?

JANE   I guess so . . .

SLIM   (*Chuckles softly*) What'sa matter? (*Gently*) Getting homesick already?

JANE   No.

SLIM   No?

JANE   (*Defiantly*) No!

SLIM   Okay, okay. So you're not getting homesick . . . I just thought maybe you were sounding that way.

JANE   (*Almost brokenly*) Well, I'm not.

SLIM   Okay, that's fine . . . I get homesick sometimes.

JANE   You do? I thought you said you didn't have a home.

SLIM   Yeah . . . It isn't being homesick for a place, you know, not missing an actual physical place. It's more of missing the people I know . . . (*Shrugs*) I don't know — every time I stop anywhere I always wish just as I'm leaving that I wasn't. That I could stay and talk with the people I'm leaving behind just a little longer.

JANE   Well, why don't you?

SLIM   I gotta go sooner or later . . . Anyway, there's people in other places I want to see just as much. And then I always meet lots of new people.

JANE   You must know a lot of people.

SLIM Yeah, I suppose. I meet people all over. Well, look I even met you today. I bet I'm the first person you've met hitching on this trip. Right?

JANE Yes.

SLIM See, you'll know a whole bunch too, soon.

JANE D'you think so?

SLIM Yeah, sure, if you travel even for a little while, then go home. You'll be sitting home one night with nothing happening and all of a sudden you'll think to yourself, "Gee, I wonder what Joe's doing out in Cedar Junction, or some place like that". And before you know it you'll be out on the side of the road, holding out your thumb, and can hardly wait to see good old Joe. And while you're standing there watching all the cars go by, you'll start thinking back to other places you've stood at the side of the road. Why, you might even think of this time right here, wondering if we'll ever get outa' here . . . which we will, even if we have to flag down a Greyhound bus. And while you're thinking of me, well, I might even be thinking about us being here, too, only I might be at the other end of the country, standing on the side of the road coming back from somewhere . . .

JANE Or maybe you'll have found your home by then.

SLIM Yeah! Yeah! Maybe I will have . . . That's what makes it so exciting, you know. You just never know where you'll be next.

(Thunder rolls far off in the distance)

JANE Did you hear that?

SLIM Hmmmm . . . told you.

JANE (*Somewhat bashfully*) Yeah.

SLIM Good thing you thought about a raincoat. Lots of people never think about that their first trip out.

JANE This isn't my first trip, I told you.

SLIM Oh, yeah, I forgot . . .

JANE (*Shrugging shoulders*) Actually it is . . . I guess you could tell.

SLIM Oh . . . Not really. I was just guessing.

JANE No you weren't. You must have known when I first got here.

SLIM Well . . . I knew you were probably just starting out on *this* trip because your clothes are clean. Hardly any dust on them, you know . . . (JANE *looks at her clothes as he speaks*) But don't worry, like I said, a couple of days on the road and nobody'll ever know the difference.

(JANE *smiles. Thunder rolls again, still far off*)

JANE   Did you ever have a raincoat? (*Looks at* SLIM'S *sleeping bag*) You're really travelling *light*, aren't you?

SLIM   Yeah . . . make the hiking part easier . . . but I did have a raincoat, you know. Lost it just a few days ago . . . Got it stolen, actually.

JANE   Oh, no.

SLIM   Yeah. I was eating in a restaurant and somebody made off with it when I wasn't looking. Just left my sleeping bag.

JANE   Who do you think took it?

SLIM   (*Shrugs*) Coulda' been just about anybody. Another hitch-hiker, maybe. Maybe somebody who didn't like long hair . . . Run into that a lot, especially in the small towns . . . Anyway, it's gone . . .

JANE   (*Looking down the road*) What's your name?

SLIM   My name . . . Well, today I feel like a . . . (*Considers*) like a "Slim".

JANE   A Slim?

SLIM   Yeah . . . Today.

JANE   Today? You mean you change your name a lot?

SLIM   Not every day. Just when I feel like it. I was a Slim yesterday, too . . . I was a Hank for a week before that.

JANE   How long do you think you'll want to keep being a Slim?

SLIM   Hard to say. I kind of like Slim — don't you?

JANE   Ah, well . . .

SLIM   What's your name?

JANE   Jane.

SLIM   Jane . . . (*In a mysterious tone, simply to be mysterious*) Ah . . .

JANE   I see another car coming, Slim.

SLIM   Oh, yeah? (SLIM *sits up, looks down the road*) Umph . . . Muscle car. (*Leans back against the post*) Forget it . . . They never pick you up. Just single chicks.

(JANE *stands up and thumbs anyway. Car roars by off-stage.* JANE *drops her arm*)

SLIM   See what I mean? They never stop . . . Or hardly ever. I think I've had two rides from them, and both of those were in the

35

city. Those guys are always in too much of a *hurry* going nowhere . . . At least we take our time, wouldn't you say?

JANE   Yes.

(SLIM laughs. He chews on his piece of grass. JANE, tiring of looking down the road, stares at her feet, her thumbs hooked in her belt loops)

SLIM   You know what I did last time I was on the road?

JANE   What?

SLIM   I was on the road nine days.

JANE   What did you do?

SLIM   I read the Bible.

JANE   The Bible?

SLIM   Yeah. Or at least, the New Testament.

JANE   *(With some disbelief, looking at SLIM)* Yeah? . . . *You?*

SLIM   Yep. The whole thing. It was a good way to pass the time . . . This time I think I should have brought along the Old Testament.

JANE   How come you chose the Bible?

SLIM   I don't know . . . Thought it was about time I read it, I guess.

JANE   Yeah?

SLIM   Well . . . I met this woman once in a place out west, who was really heavy on the whole thing, and I used to argue with her whether it's meant to be taken literally, word for word . . . She said it was, and I said it wasn't . . . In fact, I argued with her mainly just to give her static . . . But I always lost because she could out-quote me . . . everytime . . . so this time when I see her maybe I'll win a little, too.

JANE   Is that where you're going now? To see her?

SLIM   Yeah, I'll see her. Passing through her town, you know, and I'll stay a while, but I'll keep going after we've thrashed our little minds about for a while . . . But you know what I found out?

JANE   What?

SLIM   From reading the Bible, I mean.

JANE   Yeah. What?

SLIM   Well — have you ever read the Bible?

JANE   Little bits. Never all of it — —

SLIM   Yeah, well, that's just like I was — a little quote here, a little quote there. Right?

JANE   Right.

SLIM   I read it, and I discovered that Christ was different than what people make him out to be.

JANE   You mean he was better?

SLIM   No . . . No, it seemed to me he wasn't as great as people make him out to be . . . There seemed to be a lot more — superstition in there that I really hadn't counted on.

JANE   Is that right?

SLIM   Yep . . . I think I'll have to read it again. That can't be right.

(A car suddenly roars by and is gone before they know it)

JANE   I didn't even see that one coming.

SLIM   No matter, Jane. It was a Cadillac.

(SLIM gets to his feet, looks down the road)

SLIM   Some cars never pick you up. Cadillacs, for one.

(SLIM begins wandering about, gesturing with one hand, the thumb on the other hand hooked in his belt)

SLIM   Mustangs and Barracudas are some more. You can usually forget Oldsmobiles, Mercedez-Benz and Jaguars, too. Write off the little old ladies and little old men, too, except for once when I got picked up by an old guy in a pink Studebaker who drove 85 the whole way to his farm, which was nice of him even if he did let me out in the middle of nowhere and I had to walk seven miles to the next town.

(SLIM takes his thumb out of his belt, places his hand on his hip)

SLIM   Evidently we can forget the Ramblers and the Volvos and the Volkswagens today, too. *(Stares down highway, rubs stomach)* Gees, I'm hungry . . .

JANE   I have an apple in my pack.

SLIM   You have? Apple'd go real well right now.

James Tallman

(JANE *opens her pack, gets him an apple, hands it to him*)

SLIM   Thank you, Jane . . . When we get to a cafe I'll buy you lots of
      growlies.
JANE   Growlies?
SLIM   Yeah, growlies . . . you know, food. Haven't you ever listened
      to your stomach when it's hungry? It goes "growly-growly".

(They laugh)

JANE   Have you got enough money?
SLIM   (*Biting into apple*) For the growlies?
JANE   Yes.
SLIM   Sure.
JANE   You don't have a job, do you?
SLIM   (*Eating apple*) Not right now . . . Get them here and there . . .
      for a few days . . . just enough to keep me in lots of growlies.

(SLIM *places the apple core carefully on the top of the sign
    post. JANE, who has been looking down the road, looks
    over at him*)

JANE   What are you doing?
SLIM   I'm putting up my sign.
JANE   Your sign?

(SLIM *stands back and looks at apple core*)

SLIM   Yeah. (JANE *laughs*) What's so funny?
JANE   An apple core as your sign?
SLIM   Sure!
JANE   What do you need with a sign!
SLIM   So people will know I've stopped here. It lets people know I
      am.
JANE   Yeah? But nobody will know who put it up there.

SLIM Well, they'll know somebody did . . . It doesn't matter if they don't know *who* put it there. (SLIM *looks at apple core*) They'll just know that somebody was here once. Maybe they'll remember the apple core next time they pass by, and then I'll be remembered, too. (SLIM *looks at* JANE) Otherwise, you see, you can pass through this country and nobody cares, nobody even knows you've *been*.

JANE Do you really think so? . . . I mean, is it so important to be remembered?

SLIM Well, see all these guys rushing past here? . . .

JANE (*Looking up and down road*) Not really.

SLIM Well, wait a while and maybe we'll see one — but they all think they're getting somewhere. They're *going* somewhere, at least. Now, they like to think they're affecting the lives of others. Maybe they do, maybe they don't. But with me, you see, I just get in their car and go as far as they're going and then I get out. I haven't affected them — I haven't *touched* them — they get to where they wanted to get. Whether they do or don't has nothing to do with me . . . They're making their mark in the world and they think it's important . . . This is mine . . .

JANE An apple core?

SLIM Yeah. People drive by and see it there, they think, "Hmm, that's a funny place for an apple core. I wonder how it got there?" — I mean, how many apple cores have you seen on the top of sign posts?

JANE Does it really matter?

(SLIM *sits down under the sign*)

SLIM It's as important as anything else, I suppose. See, for maybe twenty or thirty seconds I've affected the lives of others. People.

JANE That's as much as you can hope for, I guess.

SLIM Yeah . . .

(*A car suddenly roars past.* JANE *holds her thumb out, but she is too late. She turns and watches the car drive out of sight*)

SLIM   *There* goes one of those guys in a hurry.

(JANE *sighs. Her eye is caught by the apple core on top of the sign post*)

JANE   That apple will rot away, Slim . . . Then people will forget you were ever here.

SLIM   Well, that gives me a reason to come back, doesn't it, to put up a new sign . . .

JANE   (*Irritated*) Is that all you want to do? (*Her anger grows*) Just stand on the side of this road all your life —

SLIM   I'm not standing —

JANE   You just want to watch the cars go by and leave signs littered all over the country? Don't you want to go anywhere?

SLIM   Yes! ! Down the road! Just like those guys in their cars. (*Gestures towards highway with his thumb*)

JANE   But they've got some place to go.

SLIM   Well, I'm *looking* for a place to go! That's why I'm here. I don't think those guys even wonder or think *why* they're rushing along at seventy miles an hour. They don't know *why* they're going *where* they're going. They probably never think about it . . . At least I know *why* I'm here—

JANE   Oh, shut up!

(JANE *looks down the road, moves away from* SLIM. JANE *continues to stare down the road*)

SLIM   If the cars are coming, they're coming. There's nothing you can do about that. Just relax and wait and we'll see what comes along.

JANE   (*In controlled, angry voice, without looking at* SLIM) That's all you ever seem to do — just wait . . . No wonder you never affect anybody — you don't *do* anything to affect them . . . Just leave your stupid signs . . .

SLIM   Evidently you don't like me again . . .

JANE   Shut up!

SLIM   You're always looking down the road. Do that for too long, you'll get those lines around your eyes — crow's-feet, you know.

(JANE *does not reply, but is slightly disconcerted. She stops looking down the road. She looks over at* SLIM)

JANE I will?
SLIM Yep. In fact, I think I can see them starting there right now.
JANE (*Holding her fingers to her temples*) You can?
SLIM (*Laughs*) No. Look down the road all you want.

(JANE *rubs sides of her temples for a moment, looking at* SLIM, *pondering whether he is serious or not, then decides he's not. She has forgotten her anger, however. She looks back down the road*)

JANE (*Softly*) I guess your sign is mine, too, Slim.
SLIM (*Looking over at* JANE) What?
JANE It was my apple, remember?
SLIM (*Chuckling softly*) Yeah . . . Yeah, I guess it was.
JANE (*Looking at* SLIM) So that means it's partly my sign, too, doesn't it?
SLIM (*After thinking that over briefly*) Yeah, I guess it does, all right . . . It's *our* sign . . . our apple core.

(*Silence.* SLIM *looks at her*)

SLIM Does that mean we can be buddies again?
JANE (*Nods and smiles*) Yes.
SLIM Well . . . That gets a load off my chest. Never like to be on the road with anybody who isn't a good buddy.

(JANE *smiles to herself. A car is heard approaching*)

SLIM Here comes one.
JANE I'll take care of it. You got sore feet, remember?
SLIM Umph.

James Tallman

(JANE holds her thumb out as the car roars by. SLIM, forming a question in his mind, ignores the car's passing)

SLIM You live around here, hey, Jane?
JANE *(Looking up road after car)* Not around *here*. I live about 30 miles away. *(Turns and faces SLIM)*
SLIM Oh . . . You always lived here — I mean, there?
JANE Yes.
SLIM Hmm.
JANE I've never lived anywhere else . . . It's my home.
SLIM You know what home is, Jane?
JANE Yes . . .

(A car goes by. They simply ignore it, waiting for the noise to subside before carrying on their conversation)

JANE It's the place where you grow up . . . Where you put down roots, I guess.
SLIM It is for most people, I suppose . . . But — what if you don't grow up in the same place? What if you move around when you're still a kid? . . . You know, I never had roots anywhere.
JANE Everybody has roots . . . If you live anywhere for very long you're bound to put them down.
SLIM Yeah? . . . But how would you know? I thought you always lived in one place.
JANE Well, how can you help not put roots down?
SLIM You know where I was born?
JANE Where?
SLIM In the east . . . and I *was* starting to put down roots. But then my family moved out west.
JANE Well, didn't you put down roots there, then?
SLIM Well . . . not really. Home is — well, it's not a house — I mean, it's not just any old place where you happen to be staying . . . It's the first place where you first start to notice things — all kinds of things — people, sounds, things that happen to you. And, you see, anything that happens to you after that, or any place you ever go, you always compare it to your home — to the place where you first became *aware*. You have to have those first early impressions . . . or else you drift.

42

JANE   But everybody has first impressions.

SLIM   Yeah, but I was just getting used to my first impressions — just getting to know them — and we moved out west and everything was different — and my little mind got all confused. I couldn't remember which impressions had come first . . . couldn't remember which impressions I was supposed to use for the comparison, the yardstick . . . See what I mean?

JANE   Yeah.

SLIM   Yeah, well, don't you understand? That's why I don't stay at home — I don't know where it is. I've never really *been* home. That's why I'm out here in the sun and the rain and sleep in ditches and eat in roadside cafes . . . until I find where my home is . . . I can't rest, I can't settle down, 'til then.

JANE   Where do you think you'll find it? Or do you *ever expect* to find it?

SLIM   Oh, yeah, I hope so . . . I don't know. It must be out there somewhere . . . Somewhere a place where suddenly I *know* I belong — because I don't have to try comparing it to anywhere else, you know — it'll just feel right — I'll just sort of lock into it.

(Thunder rolls nearby)

JANE   I hope you find it.

SLIM   It could happen anytime . . . Rain's coming . . . See it? *(Points up into audience)*

JANE   Yes . . .

SLIM   *(Leaning back against post)* I'm tired of thinking for a while . . . Think I'll just lie here and feel the rain on my head.

JANE   I'll get out my raincoat and we can both get under it.

SLIM   Oh. All right. I'll lie here and *listen* to the rain instead.

(As JANE *begins to open her pack, a car approaches.* SLIM *holds out his thumb. The car slows down and stops just past them.* SLIM *looks over his shoulder upper stage left)*

SLIM   Hey! He's stopped.

James Tallman

(SLIM sits up straight. JANE looks around at car)

SLIM   Quick! Before he changes his mind.

(JANE starts doing up her pack. SLIM jumps to his feet. He sees JANE fiddling with pack)

SLIM   Never mind that, Jane! Just get in before he changes his mind!

(JANE picks up her pack and runs towards upper stage left and into darkness. SLIM collects his sleeping bag and jacket)

SLIM   Well, here we come, growlies, here we come!

(SLIM runs off into darkness, upper stage left. Car door slams, car drives away. Fade out)

After the Play Suggestions:

For Writing and Discussion

1. Jane wants to cover up the fact that she has never hitchhiked before. Why?
2. For what reasons does Slim try to "put Jane in her place" when they first meet?
3. Do you think Slim will find his "home"? Explain.
4. The apple-core is of great importance to Slim; it allows him to leave his mark. Everyone tries to leave a mark of some kind. Describe how some of your friends or family "leave their apple-cores" or personal signatures on the people around them.
5. For centuries, songs and books have been written about wanderers like Slim. Take, for example, Odysseus in *The Odyssey* by Homer. Why is the idea of the open road appealing to so many people?

For Performance

Divide the class into roughly groups of four. Then divide the script into as many sections as there are groups. Assign two members of each group to rehearse a reading of the play. The others should go to the school library, geography department or some other source and collect slides showing Canadian scenes. Prepare a multi-media show in which the slides are shown while the voices of the actors are heard over them. You might also wish to use music to make the presentation even more effective.

The Boor

by Anton Chekhov

Anton Chekhov (1860-1904) was a Russian author of short stories and plays. His work for the theatre is still produced regularly in North America and Europe. Among his best-known plays are: *The Sea Gull, Uncle Vanya, The Three Sisters* and *The Cherry Orchard*.

Anton Chekhov

Before the Play

Working in pairs at your desks, improvise the following situation:
The two most stubborn people in the world are going to a cottage.
They reach a fork in the road and can't agree on the correct way to
proceed. How do they settle it?

Characters:

HELENA IVANOVNA POPOV *A young widow, mistress of a
country estate.*
GRIGORI STEPANOVITCH SMIRNOV *Proprietor of a country
estate.*
LUKA *Servant of* MRS. POPOV.
A GARDENER
A COACHMAN
SEVERAL WORKMEN

SCENE: *A well-furnished reception room in* MRS. POPOV'S
home. MRS. POPOV *is discovered in deep mourning,
sitting upon a sofa, gazing steadfastly at a photograph.*
LUKA *is also present.*

LUKA   It isn't right, ma'am. Your're wearing yourself out! The maid
and the cook have gone looking for berries; everything that
breathes is enjoying life, even the cat knows how to be
happy — slips about the courtyard and catches birds — but
you hide yourself here in the house as though you were in a
cloister. Yes, truly, by actual reckoning you haven't left this
house for a whole year.
MRS. POPOV   And I shall never leave it — why should I? My life is
over. He lies in his grave, and I have buried myself within
these four walls. We are both dead.
LUKA   There you are again! It's too awful to listen to, so it is!
Nikolai Michailovitch is dead; it was the will of the Lord,
and the Lord has given him eternal peace. You have grieved
over it and that ought to be enough. Now it's time to stop.
One can't weep and wear mourning forever! My wife died a

few years ago. I grieved for her, I wept a whole month — and then it was over. Must one be forever singing lamentations? That would be more than your husband was worth! (*He sighs*) You have forgotten all your neighbors. You don't go out and you receive no one. We live, — you'll pardon me — like the spiders, and the good light of day we never see. All the livery is eaten by the mice — as though there weren't any more nice people in the world! But the whole neighborhood is full of gentlefolk. The regiment is stationed in Riblov — officers — simply beautiful! One can't see enough of them! Every Friday a ball, and military music every day. Oh, my dear, dear ma'am, young and pretty as you are, if you'd only let your spirits live —! Beauty can't last forever. When ten short years are over, you'll be glad enough to go out a bit and meet the officers — and then it'll be too late.

MRS. POPOV (*Resolutely*) Please don't speak of these things again. You know very well that since the death of Nikolai Michailovitch my life is absolutely nothing to me. You think I live, but it only seems so. Do you understand? Oh, that his departed soul may see how I love him! I know, it's no secret to you; he was often unjust toward me, cruel, and — he wasn't faithful, but I shall be faithful to the grave and prove to him how I can love. There, in the Beyond, he'll find me the same as I was until his death.

LUKA What is the use of all these words, when you'd so much rather go walking in the garden or order Tobby or Welikan harnessed to the trap, and visit the neighbours?

MRS. POPOV (*Weeping*) Oh!

LUKA Madam, dear Madam, what is it? In Heaven's name!

MRS. POPOV He loved Tobby so! He always drove him to the Kortschagins or the Vlassovs. What a wonderful horseman he was! How fine he looked when he pulled at the reins with all his might! Tobby, Tobby — give him an extra measure of oats today!

LUKA Yes, ma'am.

(A bell rings loudly)

MRS. POPOV (*Shudders*) What's that? I am at home to no one.

LUKA Yes, ma'am. (*He goes out, centre*)

MRS. POPOV (*Gazing at the photograph*) You shall see, Nikolai, how I can love and forgive! My love will die only with me — when my poor heart stops beating. (*She smiles through her tears*) And aren't you ashamed? I have been a good, true wife, I have imprisoned myself and I shall remain true until death, and you — you — you're not ashamed of yourself, my dear monster! You quarrelled with me, left me alone for weeks —

(LUKA *enters in great excitement*)

LUKA Oh, ma'am, someone is asking for you, insists on seeing you —

MRS. POPOV You told him that since my husband's death I receive no one?

LUKA I said so, but he won't listen, he says it is a pressing matter.

MRS. POPOV I receive no one!

LUKA I told him that, but he's a wildman, he swore and pushed himself into the room; he's in the dining-room now.

MRS. POPOV (*Excitedly*) Good. Show him in. The impudent —!

(LUKA *goes out, centre*)

MRS. POPOV What a bore people are! What can they want with me? Why do they disturb my peace? (*She sighs*) Yes, it is clear I must enter a convent. (*Meditatively*) Yes, a convent.

(SMIRNOV *enters, followed by* LUKA)

SMIRNOV (*To* LUKA) Fool, you make too much noise! You're an ass! (*Discovering* MRS. POPOV — *politely*) Madam, I have the honor to introduce myself: Lieutenant in the Artillery, retired, country gentleman Grigori Stepanovitch Smirnov! I'm compelled to bother you about an exceedingly important matter.

MRS. POPOV (*Without offering her hand*) What is it you wish?

SMIRNOV Your deceased husband, with whom I had the honor to be acquainted, left me two notes amounting to about twelve hundred rubles. Inasmuch as I have to pay the interest tomorrow on a loan from the Agrarian Bank, I should like to request, madam, that you pay me the money today.

MRS. POPOV   Twelve hundred — and for what was my husband indebted to you?

SMIRNOV   He bought oats from me.

MRS. POPOV   (*With a sigh, to* LUKA) Don't forget to give Tobby an extra measure of oats.

(LUKA *goes out*)

MRS. POPOV   (*To* SMIRNOV) If Nikolai Michailovitch is indebted to you, I shall of course pay you, but I am sorry, I haven't the money today. Tomorrow my manager will return from the city and I shall notify him to pay you what is due you, but until then I cannot satisfy your request. Furthermore, today it is just seven months since the death of my husband and I am not in a mood to discuss money matters.

SMIRNOV   And I am in the mood to fly up the chimney with my feet in the air if I can't lay hands on that interest tomorrow. They'll seize my estate!

MRS. POPOV   Day after tomorrow you will receive the money.

SMIRNOV   I don't need the money day after tomorrow, I need it today.

MRS. POPOV   I'm sorry I can't pay you today.

SMIRNOV   And I can't wait until day after tomorrow.

MRS. POPOV   But what can I do if I haven't it?

SMIRNOV   So you can't pay?

MRS. POPOV   I cannot.

SMIRNOV   Hm! Is that your last word?

MRS. POPOV   My last.

SMIRNOV   Absolutely?

MRS. POPOV   Absolutely.

SMIRNOV   Thank you. (*He shrugs his shoulders*) And they expect me to stand for all that. The toll-gatherer just now met me in the road and asked me why I was always worrying? Why in Heaven's name shouldn't I worry? I need money, I feel the knife at my throat. Yesterday morning I left my house in the early dawn and called on all my debtors. If even one of them had paid his debt! I worked the skin off my fingers! The devil knows in what sort of inn I slept: in a room with a barrel of brandy! And now at last I come here, seventy versts from

51

home, hope for a little money and all you give me is moods! Why shouldn't I worry?

MRS. POPOV   I thought I made it plain to you that my manager will return from town, and then you will get your money.

SMIRNOV   I did not come to see the manager, I came to see you. What the devil — pardon the language — do I care for your manager?

MRS. POPOV   Really, sir, I am not used to such language or such manners. I shan't listen to you any further. (*She goes out, left*)

SMIRNOV   What can one say to that? Moods! Seven months since her husband died! Do I have to pay the interest or not? I repeat the question, have I to pay the interest or not? The husband is dead and all that; the manager is — the devil with him! — travelling somewhere. Now, tell me, what am I to do? Shall I run away from my creditors in a balloon? Or knock my head against a stone wall? If I call on Grusdev he chooses to be "not at home," Iroschevitch has simply hidden himself, I have quarrelled with Kurzin and came near throwing him out of the window, Masutov is ill and this woman has — moods! Not one of them will pay up! And all because I've spoiled them, because I'm an old whiner, dish-rag! I'm too tender-hearted with them. But wait! I allow nobody to play tricks with me, the devil with 'em all! I'll stay here and not budge until she pays! Brr! How angry I am, how terribly angry I am! Every tendon is trembling with anger and I can hardly breathe! I'm even growing ill! (*He calls out*) Servant!

(*LUKA enters*)

LUKA   What is it you wish?

SMIRNOV   Bring me Kvas or water! (*LUKA goes out*) Well, what can we do? She hasn't it on hand? What sort of logic is that? A fellow stands with the knife at his throat, he needs money, he is on the point of hanging himself, and she won't pay because she isn't in the mood to discuss money matters. Woman's logic! That's why I never liked to talk to women and why I dislike doing it now. I would rather sit on a powder barrel than talk with a woman. Brr! — I'm getting cold as ice, this affair has made me so angry. I need only to see such a romantic creature from a distance to get so angry that I have cramps in the calves! It's enough to make one yell for help!

(Enter LUKA)

LUKA   *(Hands him water)* Madam is ill and is not receiving.

SMIRNOV   March! (LUKA *goes out)* Ill and isn't receiving! All right, it isn't necessary. I won't receive, either! I'll sit here and stay until you bring that money. If you're ill a week, I'll sit here a week. If you're ill a year, I'll sit here a year. As Heaven is my witness, I'll get the money. You don't disturb me with your mourning — or with your dimples. We know these dimples! *(He calls out the window)* Simon, unharness! We aren't going to leave right away. I am going to stay here. Tell them in the stable to give the horses some oats. The left horse has twisted the bridle again. *(Imitating him)* Stop! I'll show you how. Stop! *(Leaves window)* It's awful. Unbearable heat, no money, didn't sleep last night and now — mourning-dresses with moods. My head aches; perhaps I ought to have a drink. Ye-s, I must have a drink. *(Calling)* Servant!

LUKA   What do you wish?

SMIRNOV   Something to drink! (LUKA *goes out.* SMIRNOV *sits down and looks at his clothes)* Ugh, a fine figure! No use denying that. Dust, dirty boots, unwashed, uncombed, straw on my vest — the lady probably took me for a highwayman. *(He yawns)* It was a little impolite to come into a reception room with such clothes. Oh, well, no harm done. I'm not here as a guest. I'm a creditor. And there is no special costume for creditors.

LUKA   *(Entering with glass)* You take great liberty, sir.

SMIRNOV   *(Angrily)* What?

LUKA   I — I — I just —

SMIRNOV   Whom are you talking to? Keep quiet.

LUKA   *(Angrily)* Nice mess! This fellow won't leave! *(He goes out)*

SMIRNOV   Lord, how angry I am! Angry enough to throw mud at the whole world! I even feel ill! Servant!

*(*MRS. POPOV *comes in with downcast eyes)*

MRS. POPOV   Sir, in my solitude I have become unaccustomed to the human voice and I cannot stand the sound of loud talking. I beg you, please to cease disturbing my rest.

SMIRNOV   Pay me my money and I'll leave.

MRS. POPOV   I told you once, plainly, in your native tongue, that I haven't the money at hand; wait until day after tomorrow.

SMIRNOV   And I also had the honor of informing you in your native tongue that I need the money, not day after tomorrow, but today. If you don't pay me today I shall have to hang myself tomorrow.

MRS. POPOV   But what can I do if I haven't the money?

SMIRNOV   So, you are not going to pay immediately? You're not?

MRS. POPOV   I cannot.

SMIRNOV   Then I'll sit here until I get the money. (*He sits down*) You will pay day after tomorrow? Excellent! Here I stay until day after tomorrow. (*Jumps up*) I ask you, do I have to pay that interest tomorrow or not? Or do you think I'm joking?

MRS. POPOV   Sir, I beg of you, don't scream! This is not a stable.

SMIRNOV   I'm not talking about stables, I'm asking you whether I have to pay that interest tomorrow or not?

MRS. POPOV   You have no idea how to treat a lady.

SMIRNOV   Oh, yes, I have.

MRS. POPOV   No, you have not. You are an ill-bred, vulgar person! Respectable people don't speak so to ladies.

SMIRNOV   How remarkable! How do you want one to speak to you? In French, perhaps! Madame, je vous prie! Pardon me for having disturbed you. What beautiful weather we are having today! And how this mourning becomes you! (*He makes a low bow with mock ceremony*)

MRS. POPOV   Not at all funny! I think it vulgar!

SMIRNOV   (*Imitating her*) Not at all funny — vulgar! I don't understand how to behave in the company of ladies. Madam, in the course of my life I have seen more women than you have sparrows. Three times have I fought duels for women, twelve I jilted and nine jilted me. There was a time when I played the fool, used honeyed language, bowed and scraped. I loved, suffered, sighed to the moon, melted in love's torments. I loved passionately. I loved to madness, loved in every key, chattered like a magpie on emancipation, sacrificed half my fortune in the tender passion, until now the devil knows I've had enough of it. Your obedient servant will let you lead him around by the nose no more. Enough! Black eyes, passionate eyes, coral lips, dimples in cheeks, moonlight whispers, soft, modest sighs, — for all that, madam, I wouldn't pay a kopeck! I am not speaking of present company, but of women in general; from the tiniest to the greatest, they are conceited, hypocritical, chattering, odious, deceitful from top to toe; vain, petty, cruel with a maddening logic, and, (*He strikes his forehead*) in this respect, please excuse my frankness, but one sparrow is worth ten of the aforementioned petticoat-philosophers. When one sees one of the romantic creatures before him he imagines he is looking at some holy being, so wonderful that its one breath could dissolve him in a sea of a thousand charms and delights; but if one looks into the soul — it's nothing but a common crocodile. (*He seizes the arm-chair and breaks it in two*) But the worst of all is that this crocodile imagines it is a masterpiece of creation, and that it has a monopoly on all the tender passions. May the devil hang me upside down if there is anything to love about a woman! When she is in love, all she knows is how to complain and shed tears. If the man suffers and makes sacrifices she swings her train about and tries to lead him by the nose. You have the misfortune to be a woman, and naturally you know woman's nature; tell me on your honour, have you ever in your life seen a woman who was really true and faithful? Never! Only the old and the deformed are true and faithful. It's easier to find a cat with horns or a white woodcock, than a faithful woman.

MRS. POPOV   But allow me to ask, who is true and faithful in love? The man, perhaps?

SMIRNOV   Yes indeed! The man!

MRS. POPOV   The man! (*She laughs sarcastically*) The man true and faithful in love! Well, that is something *new*! (*Bitterly*) How can you make such a statement? Men true and faithful! So long as we have gone thus far, I may as well say that of all the men I have known, my husband was the best; I loved him passionately with all my soul, as only a young, sensible woman may love; I gave him my youth, my happiness, my fortune, my life. I worshipped him like a heathen. And what happened? This best of men betrayed me in every possible way. After his death I found his desk filled with love-letters. While he was alive he left me alone for months — it is horrible even to think about it — he made love to other women in my very presence, he wasted my money and made fun of my feelings — and in spite of everything, I trusted him and was true to him. And more than that: he is dead and I am still true to him. I have buried myself within these four walls and I shall wear this mourning to my grave.

55

SMIRNOV   (*Laughing disrespectfully*) Mourning! What on earth do you take me for? As if I didn't know why you wore this black domino and why you buried yourself within these four walls. Such a secret! So romantic! Some knight will pass the castle, gaze up at the windows and think to himself: "Here dwells the mysterious Tamara who, for love of her husband, has buried herself within four walls." Oh, I understand the art!

MRS. POPOV   (*Springing up*) What? What do you mean by saying such things to me?

SMIRNOV   You have buried yourself alive, but meanwhile you have not forgotten to powder your nose!

MRS. POPOV   How dare you speak so?

SMIRNOV   Don't scream at me, please, I'm not the manager. Allow me to call things by their right names. I am not a woman, and I am accustomed to speak out what I think. So please don't scream.

MRS. POPOV   I'm not screaming. It is you who are screaming. Please leave me, I beg of you.

SMIRNOV   Pay me my money and I'll leave.

MRS. POPOV   I won't give you the money.

SMIRNOV   You won't? You won't give me my money?

MRS. POPOV   I don't care what you do. You won't get a kopeck! Leave me!

SMIRNOV   As I haven't the pleasure of being either your husband or your fiancé please don't make a scene. (*He sits down*) I can't stand it.

MRS. POPOV   (*Breathing hard*) You are going to sit down?

SMIRNOV   I already have.

MRS. POPOV   Kindly leave the house!

SMIRNOV   Give me the money.

MRS. POPOV   I don't care to speak with impudent men. Leave! (*Pause*) You aren't going?

SMIRNOV   No.

MRS. POPOV   No?

SMIRNOV   No.

MRS. POPOV   Very well. (*She rings the bell*)

(*Enter* LUKA)

MRS. POPOV   Luka, show the gentleman out.

LUKA   (*Going to* SMIRNOV) Sir, why don't you leave when you are ordered? What do you want?

SMIRNOV   (*Jumping up*) Whom do you think you are talking to? I'll
    grind you to powder.
LUKA   (*Puts his hand to his heart*) Good Lord! (*He drops into a
    chair*) Oh, I'm ill, I can't breathe!
MRS. POPOV   Where is Dascha? (*Calling*) Dascha! Pelageja!
    Dascha! (*She rings*)
LUKA   They're all gone! I'm ill! Water!
MRS. POPOV   (*To* SMIRNOV) Leave! Get out!
SMIRNOV   Kindly be a little more polite!
MRS. POPOV   (*Striking her fists and stamping her feet*) You are
    vulgar! You're a boor! A monster!
SMIRNOV   What did you say?
MRS. POPOV   I said you were a boor, a monster!
SMIRNOV   (*Steps toward her quickly*) Permit me to ask what right
    you have to insult me?
MRS. POPOV   What of it? Do you think I am afraid of you?
SMIRNOV   And you think that because you are a romantic creature
    you can insult me without being punished? I challenge you!
LUKA   Merciful heaven! Water!
SMIRNOV   We'll have a duel.
MRS. POPOV   Do you think because you have big fists and a steer's
    neck I am afraid of you?
SMIRNOV   I allow no one to insult me, and I make no exception
    because you are a woman, one of the "weaker sex!"
MRS. POPOV   (*Trying to cry him down*) Boor, boor, boor!
SMIRNOV   It is high time to do away with the old superstition that it
    is only the man who is forced to give satisfaction. If there is
    equity at all let there be equity in all things. There's a limit!
MRS. POPOV   You wish to fight a duel? Very well.
SMIRNOV   Immediately.
MRS. POPOV   Immediately. My husband had pistols. I'll bring them.
    (*She hurries away, then turns*) Oh, what a pleasure it will be
    to put a bullet in your impudent head. The devil take you!
    (*She goes out*)
SMIRNOV   I'll shoot her down! I'm no fledgling, no sentimental
    young puppy. For me, there is no weaker sex!
LUKA   Oh, sir! (*Falls to his knees*) Have mercy on me, an old man,
    and go away. You have frightened me to death already, and
    now you want to fight a duel.
SMIRNOV   (*Paying no attention*) A duel. That's equity, emancipa-
    tion. That way the sexes are made equal. I'll shoot her down
    as a matter of principle. What can a person say to such a
    woman? (*Imitating her*) "The devil take you. I'll put a bullet
    in your impudent head." What can one say to that? She was

angry, her eyes blazed, she accepted the challenge. On my honour, it's the first time in my life that I ever saw such a woman.

LUKA Oh, sir. Go away. Go away!

SMIRNOV That *is* a woman. I can understand her. A real woman. No shilly-shallying, but fire, powder, and noise! It would be a pity to shoot a woman like that.

LUKA (*Weeping*) Oh, sir, go away.

(*Enter* MRS. POPOV)

MRS. POPOV Here are the pistols. But before we have our duel please show me how to shoot. I have never had a pistol in my hand before!

LUKA God be merciful and have pity upon us! I'll go and get the gardener and the coachman. Why has this horror come to us? (*He goes out*)

SMIRNOV (*Looking at the pistols*) You see, there are different kinds. There are special duelling pistols with cap and ball. But these are revolvers, Smith & Wesson, with ejectors; fine pistols! A pair like that cost at least ninety rubles. This is the way to hold a revolver. (*Aside*) Those eyes, those eyes! A real woman!

MRS. POPOV Like this?

SMIRNOV Yes, that way. Then you pull the hammer back — so — then you aim — put your head back a little. Just stretch your arm out, please. So — then press your finger on the thing like that, and that is all. The chief thing is this: don't get excited, don't hurry your aim, and take care that your hand doesn't tremble.

MRS. POPOV It isn't well to shoot inside; let's go into the garden.

SMIRNOV Yes. I'll tell you now, I am going to shoot into the air.

MRS. POPOV That is too much! Why?

SMIRNOV Because — because. That's my business.

MRS. POPOV You are afraid. Yes. A-h-h-h! No, no, my dear sir, no flinching! Please follow me. I won't rest until I've made a hole in that head I hate so much. Are you afraid?

SMIRNOV Yes, I'm afraid.

MRS. POPOV You are lying. Why won't you fight?

SMIRNOV Because — because — I — like you.

MRS. POPOV (*With an angry laugh*) You like me! He dares to say he likes me! (*She points to the door*) Go.

SMIRNOV (*Laying the revolver silently on the table, takes his hat and starts. At the door he stops a moment gazing at her silently, then he approaches her, hesitating*) Listen! Are you still angry? I was mad as the devil, but please understand me — how can I express myself? The thing is like this — such things are — (*He raises his voice*) Now, is it my fault that you owe me money? (*Grasps the back of the chair, which breaks*) The devil knows what breakable furniture you have! I like you! Do you understand? I — I'm almost in love!

MRS. POPOV Leave! I hate you.

SMIRNOV Lord! What a woman! I never in my life met one like her. I'm lost, ruined! I've been caught like a mouse in a trap.

MRS. POPOV Go, or I'll shoot.

SMIRNOV Shoot! You have no idea what happiness it would be to die in sight of those beautiful eyes, to die from the revolver in this little velvet hand! I'm mad! Consider it and decide immediately, for if I go now, we shall never see each other again. Decide — speak — I am a noble, a respectable man, have an income of ten thousand, can shoot a coin thrown into the air. I own some fine horses. Will you be my wife?

MRS. POPOV (*Swings the revolver angrily*) I'll shoot!

SMIRNOV My mind is not clear — I can't understand. Servant — water! I have fallen in love like any young man. (*He takes her hand and she cries with pain*) I love you! (*He kneels*) I love you as I have never loved before. Twelve women I jilted, nine jilted me, but not one of them all have I loved as I love you. I am conquered, lost, I lie at your feet like a fool and beg for your hand. Shame and disgrace! For five years I haven't been in love; I thanked the Lord for it, and now I am caught, like a carriage tongue in another carriage. I beg for your hand! Yes, or no? Will you? — Good! (*He gets up and goes quickly to the door*)

MRS. POPOV Wait a moment!

SMIRNOV (*Stopping*) Well?

MRS. POPOV Nothing. You may go. But — wait a moment. No, go on, go on. I hate you. Or — no: don't go. Oh, if you knew how angry I was, how angry! (*She throws the revolver on to the chair*) My finger is swollen from this thing. (*She angrily tears her handkerchief*) What are you standing there for? Get out!

SMIRNOV Farewell!

MRS. POPOV Yes, go. (*Cries out*) Why are you going? Wait — no, go!! Oh, how angry I am! Don't come too near, don't come too near — er — come — no nearer.

SMIRNOV   (*Approaching her*) How angry I am with myself! Fall in love like a school-boy, throw myself on my knees. I've got a chill! (*Strongly*) I love you. This is fine — all I needed was to fall in love. Tomorrow I have to pay my interest, the hay harvest has begun, and then you appear! (*He takes her in his arms*) I can never forgive myself.

MRS. POPOV   Go away! Take your hands off me! I hate you — you this is — (*A long kiss*)

(*Enter* LUKA *with an ax, the gardener with a rake, the coachman with a pitch-fork, and workmen with poles*)

LUKA   (*Staring at the pair*) Merciful Heavens! (*A long pause*)

MRS. POPOV   (*Dropping her eyes*) Tell them in the stable that Tobby isn't to have any oats.

After the Play Suggestions:

For Writing and Discussion

1. The appearance of Mrs. Popov's reception room is extremely important. If you were designing the set, how would you use the furniture (stage properties) to emphasize the differences between Mrs. Popov and Smirnov?
2. Why does Mrs. Popov mourn so deeply when her husband was clearly unfaithful to her?
3. Mrs. Popov is supposed to have chosen to be alone and yet she is excited when a visitor is announced. Why?
4. Why does Smirnov choose to wait when there is no hope of his getting the money on time?
5. Smirnov challenges Mrs. Popov to a duel and then announces that he will shoot into the air? Explain.
6. There is an old saying that "hatred is akin to love." What does it mean? How does it apply to Smirnov and Mrs. Popov?
7. In developing a role, actors sometimes identify their characters with animals to help them get the "feel" of a part. Choose animals that you feel represent Smirnov and Mrs. Popov. Explain your choices.

8. Imagine that you are a marriage counsellor. It is ten years after the time of the play and Mr. and Mrs. Smirnov (she was formerly Mrs. Popov) have come to you for help. Write a brief account of your conversation with them.
9. The introduction of this book states that, ". . . the action of a play (and especially a one—act play) may occupy only minutes." The humour of *The Boor* depends on the brief time in which the events take place. Explain.

For Performance

The class should separate into groups of two or three students. Have each group choose one or two pages of the play that appeals to them and then practise reading these pages until they have a good understanding of and feeling for the scene. Using cassette recorders, each group can record the section and then play it back for themselves. Can you understand what is being said? Do the emotions of the speakers seem genuine? Are any sound effects needed to enhance the scene? If you are dissatisfied with the taping, record the reading again. When you have completed the recording to your satisfaction, play it back for another group or for the entire class.

"Mother Figure"
(from *Confusions*)

by Alan Ayckbourn

Alan Ayckbourn is the author of many plays
successfully produced in London and New York.
Born in London in 1939, he has worked in the
theatre all of his adult life, as a director, actor and
playwright. Some of his more recent successes
have been: *The Norman Conquests* (1974), *Confusions* (1976), *Just Between Ourselves* (1977) and
Ten Times Table (1978).

Alan Ayckbourn

Before the Play

Interview a mother with children under the age of five. Find out what her life is like. Ask her what, if anything, she would change about her circumstances if she could. Report back to the class.

LUCY'S *sitting-room. It is a suburban room, fairly untidy, with evidence of small children. There are two doors — one to the kitchen and back door, one to the bedrooms and front door.* LUCY *hurries in from the bedrooms on her way to the kitchen. She is untidy, unmade-up, in dressing-gown and slippers.*

LUCY   *(Calling behind her)* Nicholas! Stay in your own bed and leave Sarah alone.

(The telephone rings. LUCY *goes out to the kitchen, returning at once with a glass of water)*

All right, Jamie, darling. Mummy's coming with a dinkie . . . *(As she passes the telephone, she lifts the receiver off the rest and almost immediately replaces it)* Mummy's coming, Jamie, Mummy's coming.

*(*LUCY *goes off to the bedroom with the glass)*
(The front door chimes sound. A pause, then they sound again)
*(*LUCY *returns from the bedrooms)*

Sarah! You're a naughty, naughty girl. I told you not to play with Jamie's syrup. That's for Jamie's toothipegs . . .

(The door chimes sound again)

64

(LUCY *ignores these and goes off to the kitchen. She returns almost at once with a toilet roll, hauling off handfuls of it as she goes to perform some giant mopping-up operation)*

Nicholas, if you're not in your bed by the time I come up, I shall smack your botty.

(There are two rings on the back door bell. LUCY *goes off to the bedroom)*
(A pause)
(ROSEMARY, a rather frail, mousey-looking woman, comes in from the kitchen)

ROSEMARY   *(Calling timidly)* Woo-hoo!

(LUCY returns from the bedroom)

LUCY   *(Calling as before)* Now go to sleep. At once. *(Seeing Rosemary)* Oh.
ROSEMARY   Hallo. I thought you must be in.
LUCY   *(Puzzled)* Hallo?
ROSEMARY   I thought you were in.
LUCY   Yes.
ROSEMARY   You are.
LUCY   Yes.
ROSEMARY   Hallo.
LUCY   Hallo. *(A slight pause)* Who are you?
ROSEMARY   Next door.
LUCY   What?
ROSEMARY   From next door. Mrs. Oates. Rosemary. Do you remember?
LUCY   *(Vaguely)* Oh, yes. Hallo.
ROSEMARY   Hallo. I did ring both bells but nobody seemed . . .
LUCY   No. I don't take much notice of bells.
ROSEMARY   Oh.
LUCY   I've rather got my hands full.

ROSEMARY   Oh yes. With the children, you mean? How are they?

LUCY   Fine.

ROSEMARY   All well?

LUCY   Yes.

ROSEMARY   Good. It's three you've got, isn't it?

LUCY   Yes.

ROSEMARY   Still, I expect it's time well spent.

LUCY   I haven't much option.

ROSEMARY   No.

LUCY   Well.

ROSEMARY   Oh, don't let me — if you want to get on . . .

LUCY   No.

ROSEMARY   I mean, if you were going to bed.

LUCY   Bed?

ROSEMARY   (*Indicating* LUCY's *attire*) Well . . .

LUCY   Oh, no. I didn't get dressed today, that's all.

ROSEMARY   Oh. Not ill?

LUCY   No.

ROSEMARY   Oh.

LUCY   I just wasn't going anywhere.

ROSEMARY   Oh, well . . .

LUCY   I haven't been anywhere for weeks.

ROSEMARY   That's a shame.

LUCY   I don't think I've got dressed for weeks, either.

ROSEMARY   Ah. No, well, I must say we haven't seen you. Not that we've been looking but we haven't seen you.

LUCY   No. Do you want to sit down?

ROSEMARY   Oh, thank you. Just for a minute.

LUCY   If you can find somewhere. (*She moves the odd toy*)

ROSEMARY   (*Sitting*) Yes, we were wondering if you were alright, actually. My husband and I — Terry, that's my husband — he was remarking that we hadn't seen you for a bit.

LUCY   No.

ROSEMARY   We heard the children, of course. Not to complain of, mind you, but we heard them, but we didn't see you.

LUCY   No. (*She picks up various toys during the following and puts them in the play-pen*)

ROSEMARY   Or your husband.

LUCY   No.

ROSEMARY   But then I said to Terry, if they need us they've only to ask. They know where we are. If they want to keep themselves to themselves, that's all right by us. I mean, that's why they put up that great big fence so they could keep themselves to themselves. And that's all right by us.

LUCY   Good.

ROSEMARY   And then ten minutes ago, we got this phone call.

LUCY   Phone call?

ROSEMARY   Yes. Terry answered it — that's my husband — and they say will you accept a transfer charge call from a public phone box in Middlesbrough and Terry says, hallo, that's funny, he says, who do we know in Middlesbrough and I said, not a soul and he says, well, that's funny, Terry says, well who is it? How do we know we know him? If we don't know him, we don't want to waste money talking to him but if we do, it might be an emergency and we won't sleep a wink. And the operator says, well suit yourself, take it or leave it, it's all the same to me. So we took it and it was your husband.

LUCY   Harry?

ROSEMARY   Harry, yes. Mr. Compton.

LUCY   What did he want?

ROSEMARY   Well — you. He was worried. He's been ringing you for days. He's had the line checked but there's been no reply.

LUCY   Oh.

ROSEMARY   Has it not been ringing?

LUCY   Possibly. I don't take much notice of bells. (*She goes to listen for the children*)

ROSEMARY   Oh. Anyway, he sounded very worried. So I said I'd pop round and make sure. I took his number in case you wanted to . . .

(LUCY *is clearly not listening*)

Are you all right?

LUCY   Yes, I was listening for Nicholas.

ROSEMARY   Oh. That's the baby?

LUCY   No.

ROSEMARY   (*Warmly*) Ah.

LUCY   I'm sorry. I'm being very rude. It's just I haven't — spoken to anyone for days. My husband isn't home much.

ROSEMARY   Oh, I quite understand. Would you like his number?

LUCY   What?

ROSEMARY   Your husband's telephone number in Middlesbrough. Would you like it? He said he'd hang on. It's from a hotel.

LUCY   No.

ROSEMARY   Oh.

LUCY   Whatever he has to say to me, he can say to my face or not at all.

ROSEMARY   Ah. (*Laying a slip of paper gingerly on the coffee-table*) Well, it's there.
LUCY   Would you care for a drink or something?
ROSEMARY   A drink? Oh — well — what's the time? Well — I don't know if I should. Half past — oh yes, well — why not? Yes please. Why not? A little one.
LUCY   Orange or lemon?
ROSEMARY   I beg your pardon?
LUCY   Orange juice or lemon juice? Or you can have milk.
ROSEMARY   Oh, I see. I thought you meant . . .
LUCY   Come on. Orange or lemon? I'm waiting.
ROSEMARY   Is there a possibility of some coffee?
LUCY   No.
ROSEMARY   Oh.
LUCY   It'll keep you awake. I'll get you an orange, it's better for you.
ROSEMARY   Oh . . .
LUCY   (*As she goes*) Sit still. Don't run around. I won't be a minute.
(LUCY *goes out into the kitchen*)

(ROSEMARY *sits nervously. She rises after a second, looks guiltily towards the kitchen and sits again. The door chimes sound.* ROSEMARY *looks towards the kitchen. There is no sign of* LUCY. *The door chimes sound again.* ROSEMARY *gets up hesitantly*)

ROSEMARY   (*Calling*) Mrs. — er . . .
LUCY   (*Off, in the kitchen*) Wait, wait, wait! I'm coming . . .

(*The door chimes sound again*)
(ROSEMARY *runs off to the front door.* LUCY *returns from the kitchen with a glass of orange juice*)

Here we are, Rosemary, I . . . (*She looks round the empty room, annoyed. Calling*) Rosemary! It's on the table.

(LUCY *puts the orange juice on the coffee-table and goes out to the kitchen again.* ROSEMARY *returns from the hall with* TERRY, *a rather pudgy man in shirt sleeves*)

ROSEMARY   (sotto voce) Come in a minute.
TERRY   I'm watching the telly.
ROSEMARY   Just for a minute.
TERRY   I wondered where you'd got to. I mean, all you had to do was give her the number . . .
ROSEMARY   I want you to meet her. See what you think. I don't think she's well.
TERRY   How do you mean?
ROSEMARY   She just seems . . .
TERRY   Is she ill?
ROSEMARY   I don't know . . .
TERRY   Well, either she's ill or she isn't.
ROSEMARY   Ssh.

(LUCY returns from the kitchen with a plate of biscuits)

LUCY   Here we are now. (Seeing TERRY) Oh.
TERRY   Evening.
LUCY   Hallo.
ROSEMARY   My husband.
LUCY   Terry, isn't it?
TERRY   Yes.
LUCY   That's a nice name, isn't it? (Pointing to the sofa) Sit down there then. Have you got your orange juice, Rosemary?

(TERRY sits)

ROSEMARY   Yes, thank you. (She picks up the glass of orange juice and sits)
TERRY   Orange juice?
ROSEMARY   Yes.
TERRY   What are you doing drinking that?
ROSEMARY   I like orange juice.
LUCY   Now, here's some very special choccy bics but you mustn't eat them all. I'm going to trust you. (She starts tidying up again)
ROSEMARY   (Still humouring her) Lovely. (She mouths "say something" to TERRY)
TERRY   Yes. Well, how are you keeping then — er, sorry, I'm forgetting. Lesley, isn't it?

69

LUCY   Mrs. Compton

TERRY   Yes. Mrs. Compton. How are you?

LUCY   I'm very well, thank you, Terry. Nice of you to ask.

TERRY   And what about Har — Mr. Compton?

LUCY   Very well. When I last saw him. Rosemary dear, try not to make all that noise when you drink.

ROSEMARY   Sorry.

TERRY   Yes, we were saying that your husband's job obviously takes him round and about a lot.

LUCY   Yes. (*She starts folding nappies*)

TERRY   Doesn't get home as much as he'd like, I expect.

LUCY   I've no idea.

TERRY   But then it takes all sorts. Take me, I'm home on the nose six o'clock every night. That's the way she wants it. Who am I . . .? (*Pause*) Yes, I think I could quite envy your husband, sometimes. Getting about a bit. I mean, when you think about it, it's more natural. For a man. His natural way of life. Right back to the primitive. Woman stays in the cave, man the hunter goes off roving at will. Mind you, I think the idea originally was he went off hunting for food. Different sort of game these days, eh?

ROSEMARY   (*Hissing*) Terry!

TERRY   Be after something quite different these days, eh? (*He nods and winks*)

LUCY   Now don't get silly, Terry.

TERRY   What? Ah — beg your pardon.

(*A pause.* TERRY *munches a biscuit.* ROSEMARY *sips her orange juice*)

ROSEMARY   Very pleasant orange juice.

LUCY   Full of vitamin C.

TERRY   No, I didn't want to give you the wrong impression there. But seriously, I was saying to Rosie here, you can't put a man in a cage. You try to do that, you've lost him. See my point?

LUCY   That can apply to women, too, surely?

ROSEMARY   Yes, quite right.

TERRY   What do you mean, quite right?

ROSEMARY   Well . . .

TERRY   You're happy enough at home, aren't you?

ROSEMARY   Yes, but — yes — but . . .

TERRY   Well then, that's what I'm saying. You're the woman, you're happy enough at home looking after that. I'm the man, I have to be out and about.

ROSEMARY   I don't know about that. You'd never go out at all unless I pushed you.

TERRY   What do you mean? I'm out all day.

ROSEMARY   Only because you have to be. You wouldn't be if you didn't have to be. When you don't, you come in, sit down, watch the television and go to bed.

TERRY   I have to relax.

ROSEMARY   You're always relaxing.

TERRY   Don't deny me relaxing.

ROSEMARY   I don't.

TERRY   Yes, you do, you just said . . .

LUCY   Now, don't quarrel. I won't have any quarreling.

TERRY   Eh?

ROSEMARY   Sorry.

LUCY   Would you like an orange drink as well, Terry? Is that what it is?

TERRY   Er . . . Oh no — I don't go in for that sort of drink much, if you know what I mean. (*He winks, then reaches for a biscuit*) I'll have another one of these though, if you don't mind?

LUCY   Just a minute, how many have you had?

TERRY   This is my second. It's only my second.

LUCY   Well, that's all. No more after that. I'll get you some milk. You better have something that's good for you.

TERRY   (*Half rising*) Oh no — thank you, not milk, no.

LUCY   (*Going to the kitchen*) Wait there. (*Seeing* TERRY *has half risen*) And don't jump about while you're eating, Terry.

(LUCY *goes out to the kitchen*)

TERRY   You're right. She's odd.

ROSEMARY   I said she was.

TERRY   No wonder he's gone off.

ROSEMARY   Perhaps that's why she's odd.

TERRY   Why?

ROSEMARY   Because he's gone off.

TERRY   Rubbish. And we'll have less of that, too, if you don't mind.

ROSEMARY   What?

TERRY   All this business about me never going out of the house.

71

ROSEMARY   It's true.

TERRY   It's not true and it makes me out to be some bloody idle loafer.

ROSEMARY   All I said . . .

TERRY   And even if it is true, you have no business saying it in front of other people.

ROSEMARY   Oh, honestly, Terry, you're so touchy. I can't say a thing right these days, can I?

TERRY   Very little. Now you come to mention it.

ROSEMARY   Niggle, niggle, niggle. You keep on at me the whole time. I'm frightened to open my mouth these days. I don't know what's got into you lately. You're in a filthy mood from the moment you get up till you go to bed . . .

TERRY   What are you talking about?

ROSEMARY   Grumbling and moaning . . .

TERRY   Oh, shut up.

ROSEMARY   You're a misery to live with these days, you really are.

TERRY   I said, shut up.

ROSEMARY   (*More quietly*) I wish to God you'd go off somewhere sometimes, I really do.

TERRY   Don't tempt me. I bloody feel like it occasionally, I can tell you.

ROSEMARY   (*Tearfully*) Oh, lovely . . .

TERRY   If you think I enjoy spending night after night sitting looking at you . . . (*He throws the biscuit down*) What am I eating these damn things for . . . you're mistaken. (*Thirsty from the biscuits, he grabs her orange juice glass and drains it in one*)

ROSEMARY   That's mine, do you mind. (*She rises and stamps her foot*)

TERRY   Come on. Let's go. (*He jumps up*)

ROSEMARY   That was my orange juice when you've quite finished.

(*LUCY enters with a glass of milk*)

LUCY   Now what are you doing jumping about?

(*ROSEMARY sits*)

TERRY   We've got to be going, I'm sorry.

LUCY   Not till you've finished. Sit down.

TERRY   Listen, I'm sorry we . . .

LUCY   (Seeing ROSEMARY'S distraught state) What's the matter with Rosemary?

ROSEMARY   (Sniffing) Nothing . . .

TERRY   Nothing.

LUCY   What have you been doing to her?

TERRY   Nothing.

LUCY   Here's your milk.

TERRY   Thank you.

LUCY   You don't deserve it.

TERRY   I don't want it.

LUCY   Don't be tiresome.

TERRY   I hate the damned stuff.

LUCY   I'm not going to waste my breath arguing with you, Terry. It's entirely up to you if you don't want to be big and strong.

TERRY   Now, look . . .

LUCY   If you want to be a little weakling, that's up to you. Just don't come whining to me when all your nails and teeth fall out. Now then, Rosemary, let's see to you. (She puts down the milk, and picks up the biscuits) Would you like a choccy biccy?

ROSEMARY   No, thank you.

LUCY   Come on, they're lovely choccy, look. Milk choccy . . .

ROSEMARY   No, honestly.

TERRY   Rosie, are you coming or not?

LUCY   Well, have a drink, then. Blow your nose and have a drink, that's a good girl. (Seeing the glass) Oh, it's all gone. You've drunk that quickly, haven't you?

ROSEMARY   I didn't drink it. He did.

LUCY   What?

ROSEMARY   He drank it.

LUCY   Terry, did you drink her orange juice?

TERRY   Look, there's a programme I want to watch . . .

LUCY   Did you drink Rosemary's orange juice?

TERRY   Look, good night . . .

ROSEMARY   Yes, he did.

LUCY   Well, I think that's really mean.

ROSEMARY   He just takes anything he wants.

LUCY   Really mean.

ROSEMARY   Never thinks of asking.

TERRY   I'm going.

LUCY   Not before you've apologized to Rosemary.

TERRY   Good night.

(TERRY *goes out*)

LUCY (*Calling after him*) And don't you dare come back until you're ready to apologize. (*To* ROSEMARY) Never mind him. Let him go. He'll be back.

ROSEMARY That's the way to talk to him.

LUCY What?

ROSEMARY That's the way he ought to be talked to more often.

LUCY I'm sorry. I won't have that sort of behaviour. Not from anyone.

ROSEMARY He'll sulk now. For days.

LUCY Well, let him. It doesn't worry us, does it?

ROSEMARY No. It's just sometimes — things get on top of you — and then he comes back at night — and he starts on at me and I . . . (*She cries*) Oh dear — I'm sorry — I didn't mean to . . .

LUCY (*Cooing*) Come on now. Come on . . .

ROSEMARY I've never done this. I'm sorry . . .

LUCY That's all right. There, there.

ROSEMARY I'm sorry. (*She continues to weep*)

LUCY Look who's watching you.

ROSEMARY Who?

LUCY (*Picking up a doll*) Mr. Poddle. Mr. Poddle's watching you. (*She holds up the doll*) You don't want Mr. Poddle to see you crying, do you? Do you?

ROSEMARY (*Lamely*) No . . .

LUCY Do we, Mr. Poddle? (*She shakes Mr. Poddle's head*) No, he says, no. Stop crying, Rosie. (*She nods Mr. Poddle's head*) Stop crying, Rosie. Yes — yes.

(ROSEMARY *gives an embarrassed giggle*)

That's better. Was that a little laugh, Mr. Poddle? Was that a little laugh?

(LUCY *wiggles Mr. Poddle about, bringing him close up to* ROSEMARY'S *face and taking him away again*)

Was that a little laugh? Was that a little laugh? Was that a little laugh?

(ROSEMARY *giggles uncontrollably*)
(TERRY *enters from the hall and stands amazed*)

TERRY Er . . .

(LUCY *and* ROSEMARY *become aware of him*)

Er — I've locked myself out.
LUCY Have you come back to apologize?
TERRY You got the key, Rosie?
ROSEMARY Yes.
TERRY Let's have it then.
LUCY Not until you apologize.
TERRY Look, I'm not apologizing to anyone. I just want the key. To get back into my own house, if you don't mind. Now, come on.
ROSEMARY (*Producing the key from her bag*) Here.
LUCY Rosemary, don't you dare give it to him.
TERRY Eh?
ROSEMARY What?
LUCY Not until he apologizes.
TERRY Rosie, give me the key.
LUCY No, Rosemary. I'll take it. Give it to me.
TERRY Rosie.
LUCY Rosemary.
ROSEMARY (*Torn*) Er . . .
LUCY (*Very fiercely*) Rosemary, will you give me that key at once.

(ROSEMARY *gives* LUCY *the key*. TERRY *regards* LUCY)

TERRY Would you mind most awfully giving me the key to my own front door?
LUCY Certainly.
TERRY Thank you so much.
LUCY Just as soon as you've apologized to Rosemary.
TERRY I've said, I'm not apologizing to anyone.
LUCY Then you're not having the key.
TERRY Now listen, I've got a day's work to do tomorrow. I'm damned if I'm going to start playing games with some frustrated nutter . . .
TERRY Terry . . .
LUCY Take no notice of him, Rosemary, he's just showing off.
TERRY Are you going to give me that key or not?
LUCY Not until you apologize.
TERRY All right. I'll have to come and take it off you, won't I?
LUCY You try. You just dare try, my boy.
TERRY All right. (*He moves towards* LUCY)

ROSEMARY   Terry . . .

LUCY   Just you try and see what happens.

TERRY   (*Halted by her tone; uncertainly*) I'm not joking.

LUCY   Neither am I.

TERRY   Look, I don't want to . . . Just give me the key, there's a good . . .

LUCY   Not until you apologize to Rosemary.

TERRY   Oh, for the love of . . . All right (*To* ROSEMARY) Sorry.

LUCY   Say it nicely.

TERRY   I'm very sorry, Rosie. Now give us the key, for God's sake.

LUCY   When you've drunk your milk. Sit down and drink your milk.

TERRY   Oh, blimey . . . (*He sits*)

LUCY   That's better.

TERRY   I hate milk.

LUCY   Drink it up.

(TERRY *scowls and picks up the glass.* ROSEMARY, *unseen by* LUCY, *sticks her tongue out at him.* TERRY *bangs down his glass and moves as if to hit her*)

Terry!

TERRY   She stuck her tongue out at me.

LUCY   Sit still.

TERRY   But she . . .

LUCY   Sit!

(TERRY *sits scowling.* ROSEMARY *smirks at him smugly*)

(*Seeing her*) And don't do that, Rosemary. If the wind changes, you'll get stuck like it. And sit up straight and don't slouch.

(ROSEMARY *does so*)

TERRY   (*Taking a sip of the milk*) This is horrible.

(*Silence. He takes another sip*)

It's warm.

(*Silence. Another sip*)

TERRY   There's a football international on television, you know.

LUCY   Not until you've drunk that up, there isn't. Come on, Rosemary. Help Terry to drink it. "Georgie Porgie Pudding and Pie, Kissed the girls and . . .?"

ROSEMARY   "Made them cry."

76

LUCY   Good.
ROSEMARY   "When the boys came out to play,   *(Speaking*
LUCY   Georgie Porgie ran away."   *together)*
TERRY   *(Finishing his glass with a giant swallow)* All gone. *(He wipes his mouth)*
LUCY   Good boy.
TERRY   Can I have the key now, please?
LUCY   Here you are.

(TERRY goes to take it)

What do you say?
TERRY   Thank you.
LUCY   All right. Off you go, both of you.
ROSEMARY   *(Kissing her on the cheek)* Night night.
LUCY   Night night, dear. Night night, Terry.
TERRY   *(Kissing Lucy likewise)* Night night.
LUCY   Sleep tight.
TERRY   Hope the bugs don't bite.
LUCY   Hold Rosemary's hand, Terry.

(ROSEMARY and TERRY hold hands)

See her home safely.
TERRY   Night.
ROSEMARY   Night.
LUCY   Night night.

(TERRY and ROSEMARY go off hand in hand. LUCY blows kisses)

(With a sigh) Blooming kids. Honestly.

(The telephone rings. LUCY as she passes it, picks it up and replaces it as before. As she does so, the Lights fade to a single spot in a call-box. HARRY is there, with the receiver in his hand)

HARRY   Oh, blast not again. Hallo — hallo — oh, damn and blast. *(He jiggles the receiver)* Operator? Operator? Hallo — hallo . . . Operator, there must be a fault on this line. . . . The line I have been trying unsuccessfully to dial. . . . Yes — six-four-one-nine. I mean, this is quite unforgivable. This is the third time I have reported it and I am still quite unable to make contact with my wife. . . . Yes, well, thank you for your sympathy. Let's try a little action, shall we? Because I'm going to take this to the top. . . . Yes, top. . . . What? . . . No — T for Toffee, O for Orange. . . . Oh, forget it. (*He rings off*) Give me strength.

(HARRY *moves out of the box. As he does so, the Lights come up to full, and the set has now changed to —*)

• • •

After the Play Suggestions:

For Writing and Discussion

1. Lucy doesn't take "much notice of bells." Why not?
2. Why does Rosemary allow Lucy to turn her into a child again?
3. Why is Terry unable to take the key away from Lucy?
4. Does the playwright give any hints that Terry will finally surrender to Lucy?
5. Properties are extremely important in this play.
   (a) How, as an actor/actress would you show Terry's changing feelings by the way he treats his glass of milk?
   (b) How would you convey Lucy's situation by the way in which she folds diapers and picks up toys?
6. Is the playwright making fun of young mothers? Explain your answer.

For Improvisation

Working in pairs, complete the telephone call from Lucy's absent husband, Harry. How would they talk to each other? Show your interpretation of the telephone conversation to one other pair of students.

For Presentation

1. Divide the script so that everyone in the class has something to do either individually or as part of a group (longer scenes may be divided, shorter ones combined).
2. Assign one group to turn a corner of your classroom into a stage set. Make it as much like Lucy's living room as time and materials will allow.
3. If there is enough time, learn the lines so that you don't have to use the script. Then "block" the actions of the actors and actresses so that each knows his or her position and part in the performance.
4. When all the groups are ready, perform the play continuously in the following manner: As each pair or group of three finishes its part, the members freeze in their last position. While they hold these poses, the next group comes and freezes beside them, imitating what they see. The first group now quickly leaves the stage and the play resumes with this second group performing.

Hints:

(a) Consider carefully what your character wants or is trying to do in the scene.
(b) Costumes, if thought about carefully, will increase the effect of the presentation. How does a person's dress reflect their situation?
(c) As the groups rehearse, try to notice how others are interpreting your part.
(d) Remember to plan your scenes so that you are always facing your audience.
(e) To make sure that you can be heard, imagine that your audience is at least thirty metres away.
(f) When you're in front of the class *slow down*. Nervousness can turn you into a speed demon.
(g) *Don't* try to use the script until you have carried out the interviews suggested in the "Before the Play" activity.

Passacaglia

by Joan Mason Hurley

Passacaglia was first broadcast over CBC Radio on March 4, 1973. The first stage performance was given by the Emerald Players at the Greater Vancouver Zone of the British Columbia Drama Festival, April 23, 1973. The play won Best Original Script Award at the British Columbia Drama Association Finals at Prince George, British Columbia, in June 1973.

Joan Mason Hurley was born in Victoria, and has lived most of her life in British Columbia. More than a dozen of her stage plays have been produced in the last ten years. Her work has been performed on stages in Canada and England, and on the CBC.

Joan Mason Hurley

Before the Play

1. Interview residents of a home for "senior citizens" to find out as much as possible about their lives and present lifestyles. Plan your questions in advance and record the answers on paper or on tape.
2. Set up your classroom like a retirement home. Have half the class circulate around the room interviewing the other half of the class, the latter acting the parts of the residents of this home. The "residents" should make use of the information gathered from doing question 1. Now switch roles of interviewer and resident, and continue with the interviewing.

It is approaching the hour for morning coffee in the living room at Fairview Manor, retirement home. A very old woman of emaciated and eccentric appearance is seated in a rocking chair DOWN LEFT absorbed in swatting flies. A tattered envelope is the repository of her victims. Her name is GIBBS. *On the opposite side of the room* MISS FANSHAWE, *vigorous and upright, is playing solitaire.*

GIBBS   Gottcha. Hey, Fanny, Fanny! Hear me, Fanny!
FANSHAWE   Miss Gibbs, my name is Fanshawe.
GIBBS   Speak up. Can't hear you so good, Fanny.
FANSHAWE   (*Shouts*) I said I will not be called Fanny.

(MATRON *enters followed by* NANCY *pushing a trolley. Both are wearing uniforms*)

MATRON   (*Forced cheerfulness*) Good morning, ladies. Coffee time.
FANSHAWE   Matron, that woman is intolerable.
MATRON   Oh, Miss Fanshawe, not again.
FANSHAWE   What do you mean? It's hardly *my* fault.
MATRON   I've advised you to pay no attention.
FANSHAWE   That's hardly possible. And who is this girl, pray?

NANCY   Good morning. My name is Nancy.
GIBBS   Hey, Fan–ny. I got three. Three dead.
FANSHAWE   Stark, raving, mad.
GIBBS   Pay no 'tention, Fanny.
MATRON   Now, Miss Gibbs. That's *enough*.
GIBBS   Eh?
MATRON   Stop teasing Miss Fanshawe, there's a good girl.
GIBBS   (*Cackling*) No, I'm bad girl.
FANSHAWE   She's senile, of course. (*To* NANCY) Even you can see
   that.
NANCY   I think she's kind of sweet.
FANSHAWE   Do you, indeed.
GIBBS   (*Swats fly*) Gottcha.
NANCY   And simply fantastic at catching flies.
MATRON   Yes, Miss Gibbs keeps us absolutely free of flies.
FANSHAWE   An accomplishment accounted for, I believe, because
   she used to keep a bakery.
GIBBS   (*Chanting*) Raisins and currants, flies in the buns, Fanny.
   Flies in the buns.
MATRON   Miss Gibbs, that will *do*.

(NANCY *takes coffee to* FANSHAWE *on a tray which holds
   cream jug, sugar basin and a plate of biscuits*)

FANSHAWE   (*To* NANCY) You look very young to be a nurse.

(FANSHAWE *very deliberately helps herself to cream and sugar
   and takes a biscuit*)

NANCY   I'm not a nurse, Miss Fanshawe.
MATRON   Nancy's just here to help.
FANSHAWE   Well it makes very little difference to me what she's
   here for. I don't require assistance.
MATRON   You enjoy wonderful health.
FANSHAWE   And if I didn't I would take an overdose. Euthanasia,
   self-administered, and my body to medical research.
MATRON   (*Taking coffee to* GIBBS) Oh, Miss Fanshawe, you
   shouldn't talk like that.
FANSHAWE   Why not, plain fact. Well, girl, cat got your tongue?
NANCY   No.

MATRON   Nancy's young and everything's a little strange yet.

FANSHAWE   Strange?

NANCY   Yes. You see I've never worked in an old persons' home before.

FANSHAWE   Well, Matron! So much for Fairview Manor with its dignity, security and happiness.

MATRON   Nancy, whatever are you thinking about?

NANCY   I'm sorry. I didn't mean to say the wrong thing.

GIBBS   (*Cackling*) Old persons. Tee hee, that's us. Old persons, Fanny.

MATRON   Nancy, Fairview Manor is not an old persons' home, and our residents are guests. Kindly remember that in future.

NANCY   Yes, Matron.

(Telephone rings)

MATRON   Please answer that.

(Exit NANCY)

FANSHAWE   Old persons' home, indeed. The girl's a fool.

MATRON   Just inexperienced. She'll learn.

FANSHAWE   I doubt it. And if you ask me she won't be staying around here long.

MATRON   Oh, I do hope so. We're so under-staffed, quite run off our feet. Why it's a job just to keep the place clean.

FANSHAWE   It hasn't escaped my notice, even the cards are filthy. (*Indicating*) Considering the money they charge here, you'd think they could supply clean ones.

MATRON   I'll see what can be done.

FANSHAWE   And how much longer must this jigsaw puzzle clutter up the table?

MATRON   (*Walking over to look*) Hasn't Mrs. Rose finished it yet?

FANSHAWE   No, she has not.

MATRON   And I don't suppose she'll get much done today.

FANSHAWE   The usual carnations, and the usual fuss, I suppose. One would think she was the only person who ever had a birthday.

MATRON   But this one is special. Today her granddaughter comes.

FANSHAWE   She's only mentioned it ten thousand times. I pity the girl. All us old women. Most depressing.

(Enter MRS. MARTELLI *carrying a knitting bag. She has a kind, intelligent face and walks with a white cane, but firmly, as if she knew where she was going)*

MARTELLI   Depressing? Not talking about me, Miss Fanshawe? Blind, I may be, but depressing, I hope not.
MATRON   Here's your chair, Mrs. Martelli, in its usual place.

*(*MRS. MARTELLI *goes directly to it and sits down. She hooks her cane over the arm and places her knitting bag on the floor)*

MARTELLI   Thank you, Matron. Have you heard whether the concert in the park will be broadcast this afternoon?
MTRON   I looked in the paper, it wasn't mentioned.

*(*MATRON *pours coffee, hands it to* MARTELLI*)*

MARTELLI   Disappointing. I did hope to hear the Pastoral Symphony.
FANSHAWE   The Pastoral Symphony's been played to death.
MARTELLI   *(Mildly)* Your opinion, Miss Fanshawe?
GIBBS   *(Swats fly)* Gottcha. Number Five.
MARTELLI   *(Hearing her)* Is that you, Miss Gibbs. I have my radio back. *(Feels her Braille watch)* I won't forget the weather.
GIBBS   Feather. What feather?
MARTELLI   I said, I won't forget the weather.
MATRON   It's no use, Mrs. Martelli. She can't hear.
MARTELLI   Yes, she can. She can hear when she wants to. And I like to include her. It's friendly.

(She ''looks'' in the direction of MISS FANSHAWE. NANCY *enters)*

NANCY   It was the drugstore calling, Matron. They're sending up Mrs. Rose's prescription after lunch. *(She hands a pile of letters to* MATRON*)* And the mail came. I brought it in.
*(*MATRON *begins to sort mail)*
MARTELLI   That's a new voice.
NANCY   *(Brightly)* Good morning. I'm Nancy.

85

(MRS. MARTELLI *holds out her hand, waits for* NANCY *to take it*)

MARTELLI   Come and shake hands with me, Nancy. Ah, what a smooth young hand. How old are you, child?

NANCY   Nineteen, m'am.

MARTELLI   Nineteen? And you're shutting yourself up with us old crocks?

FANSHAWE   Speak for yourself, Mrs. Martelli.

NANCY   I don't live in. It's only an eight hour shift.

MARTELLI   Only an eight hour shift? Well, well.

MATRON   Here's a circular for you, Miss Fanshawe, from St. Hilda's School.

FANSHAWE   I can see for myself where it's from, Matron.

MARTELLI   Matron, are you looking through the mail? Is there one for Mrs. Rose?

MATRON   I'm afraid not. Only bills, and two for upstairs.

MARTELLI   Oh dear. I did so hope her son would write for her birthday.

MATRON   Perhaps she'll hear tomorrow.

FANSHAWE   She won't. You know he never writes.

MARTELLI   Well, I understand he's a very busy man.

MATRON   And I'm a busy woman. Mrs. Jenkins has been waiting for this letter. You might water the plants, Nancy, and if the doorbell goes, answer it, it may be the prescription.

NANCY   Yes, Matron.

MATRON   Call me if you need me, I'll be upstairs. Mercy on us, next thing you know it'll be lunch.

(*Exit* MATRON)

GIBBS   Lunch? I'm hungry. What's for lunch?

MARTELLI   It's Friday.

GIBBS   Fried eggs?

MARTELLI   No, Friday. Fish.

GIBBS   Fish! Yee–uck.

FANSHAWE   Impossible woman.

MARTELLI   Her money's as good as ours.

FANSHAWE   How she affords it, I don't know. She had a bakeshop, if you please.

MARTELLI You mention the fact rather frequently, Miss Fanshawe; and you were a school marm, and I played the piano. But it's hardly relevant now, is it? Nancy, are you still there? Be a dear and help me with my knitting. I've dropped a stitch and can't seem to pick it up.

NANCY (*Admiring*) What a lovely shawl.

FANSHAWE Flattery!

MARTELLI You won't deny it's useful.

NANCY (*Rubbing it against her cheek*) Mm. So warm. Lovely.

(She sits on stool, starts to pick up stitch)

MARTELLI I make them for the Salvation Army. It gives me an occupation. I like to be of use to those less fortunate than myself.

NANCY Less fortunate, did you say?

MARTELLI Yes, my dear. I've been sighted most of my life.

(Enter MRS. ROSE in a wheelchair. She is wearing a dressing gown)

ROSE (*Gaily*) Morning, everybody, morning.

(Accidentally she bumps FANSHAWE'S table)

FANSHAWE Watch where you're going, Mrs. Rose.

ROSE Sorry. I'd never pass my driver's test, would I? But here's a new face. Matron didn't tell us we were going to have someone new. What's your name, dear?

NANCY Nancy.

MARTELLI Nancy's come to look after us. Well, my dear, today's the great day. Congratulations.

(NANCY gives knitting back. Goes to trolley)

ROSE Thank you, dear. I'm very excited.

FANSHAWE You look it. Your face is positively red. You'll be having another one of your attacks if you don't watch out.

ROSE Oh no. I'm feeling particularly well. Seventy-seven years old today. Don't you think that's a lucky number?

FANSHAWE I do not. And at our age making a fuss of birthdays is ridiculous. You don't hear me going on when it's mine, do you?

MARTELLI If we knew when it was, Miss Fanshawe, we'd be glad to help you celebrate.

FANSHAWE (Scornfully) Celebrate! Commiserate, don't you mean?

GIBBS (Chanting) Happy birthday to you, happy birthday to you.

ROSE Thank you, Miss Gibbs. Thank you very much.

(NANCY comes forward with coffee, etc. on a tray)

NANCY Yes, Mrs. Rose. Many happy returns.

(MRS. ROSE helps herself)

FANSHAWE Many happy returns? At seventy-seven. Absurd.

MARTELLI It's the usual greeting and no doubt kindly meant. I'm sure we all join Nancy in wishing as many more birthdays for Mrs. Rose as she, herself, would like.

ROSE As many more as I, myself, would like. How beautifully you put it. To tell you the truth, Nancy, since my hubby died I've often wished I could join him. But not today.

MARTELLI No dear, today is special.

ROSE (To NANCY) It's because today Alison comes. My grand-daughter, you know, dear. She's about your age, but I haven't seen her for sixteen years. I'm expecting her to be very pretty.

(NANCY goes back to trolley with tray)

FANSHAWE Because she's your granddaughter, I suppose?

ROSE Because she was such a lovely little girl.

FANSHAWE   People change in sixteen years. She could be plain as porridge.

NANCY   Not necessarily. (*Taking* MISS FANSHAWE'S *cup away*)

FANSHAWE   Well, Miss, and who are you to express an opinion?

NANCY   Nowadays it's personality that counts.

FANSHAWE   Young lady, I don't know who you think you're talking to, but at St. Hilda's . . .

ROSE   (*To* NANCY) Alison's named after me, you know.

NANCY   What a compliment.

ROSE   Yes. Alison is my name. And though it's so long since we've seen each other, she's always been very special to me.

FANSHAWE   You interrupted, Mrs. Rose.

MARTELLI   I'm sorry you're feeling out of sorts this morning.

FANSHAWE   Out of sorts? Me?

GIBBS   Sour grapes. Sour grapes. Fanny's got a stommick ache.

FANSHAWE   That woman is insufferable.

MARTELLI   (*With meaning*) Is she?

FANSHAWE   Why doesn't the girl take her to her room? Nancy!

MARTELLI   Don't bully, Miss Fanshawe. Matron gave no such orders.

ROSE   Is the mail in?

FANSHAWE   Yes, and there's nothing for you.

MARTELLI   Perhaps tomorrow, dear.

ROSE   Yes, perhaps tomorrow. Anyway, I have the telegram. (*Fumbles in bag*) Dear me, where is it?

GIBBS   The weather! The weather! What about the weather?

NANCY   (*Coming forward*) The weather?

MARTELLI   On the radio, Nancy. (*Feels watch*) Not quite time, Miss Gibbs. I won't forget.

ROSE   (*Finding telegram in bag*) Here it is. (*To* NANCY) Perhaps you'd like to read it, my dear. It's from my daughter-in-law, Carol. She's been a good wife for Charlie. They live in Montreal, you know. I believe they have a very nice home, move in quite the best society.

FANSHAWE   (*Sarcastically*) You must tell Nancy all about the new Cadillac, the summer place on the river and . . .

MARTELLI   Read the telegram aloud, please, Nancy.

FANSHAWE   You interrupted me again.

NANCY   ALISON ARRIVING VANCOUVER FRIDAY AIR CANADA FLIGHT EIGHT O THREE STOP. WILL HIRE U-DRIVE AIRPORT VISIT YOU BEFORE DEPARTURE SAN FRANCISCO FIVE PM SIGNED CAROL. (*Pause*) Well, that's business-like, all right, and you say you haven't seen her for sixteen years! (*She gives it back*)

ROSE   Carol is a little brisk. It's her upbringing, my dear. Always calls me Mrs. Rose. Isn't that queer? Still, I'm sure her heart's in the right place. It doesn't say what time Alison's coming, does it?

MARTELLI   You remember, dear, Matron phoned the airport and inquired.

ROSE   Oh yes. Noon, she said. About noon she'll arrive.

MARTELLI   That's right. She'll soon be here. What a lovely birthday present.

ROSE   The very nicest I could have. Just think of seeing Alison.

NANCY   Only an hour to wait, Mrs. Rose.

FANSHAWE   Then we won't have to hear that telegram again.

MARTELLI   I shall be sorry when today is over. I've been so looking forward to seeing Alison.

NANCY   To seeing her?

MARTELLI   Mrs. Rose is my eyes. She describes things beautifully.

ROSE   Thank you, dear.

FANSHAWE   I hope you don't intend to entertain the girl in here? Most unpleasant for her, a room full of old women waiting to die.

MARTELLI   (*Vigorously*) What rubbish. Who's waiting to die? Not us. I'm waiting to do the crossword. We'll have time, Mrs. Rose, before Alison comes.

GIBBS   (*Swatting a fly*) Six dead. Six this morning. Must get seven. Seven's lucky number.

FANSHAWE   (*Getting up*) What a sight. What a spectacle. I can't bear to look at her.

GIBBS   Spectacle. Spectacle. Fanny's a spectacle. Lost your spectacles, Fanny?

ROSE   (*Upset*) But I must have Alison in here. My bedroom's so small.

MARTELLI   Don't worry dear. We'll all enjoy her.

FANSHAWE   But the point is, will she enjoy us?

(MISS FANSHAWE *stalks out.* MRS. ROSE *chokes softly*)

NANCY   Are you all right, Mrs. Rose? Would you like me to call Matron?

MARTELLI   She'll be all right in a moment, Nancy. Is the paper around? Can you see it?

NANCY   Here it is.

MARTELLI   Give it to Mrs. Rose. I have a pencil in my bag.

NANCY (*Handing paper*) Don't be upset, please, Mrs. Rose. Would
you like a glass of water?

ROSE Thank you. You're a kind girl. (*Tries to smile*)

(NANCY *pours water. Hands* MRS. ROSE *a glass. She drinks*)

NANCY That better?

ROSE Yes.

(*Doorbell goes*)

NANCY Excuse me, I'll be back in a minute. (*Exits*)

MARTELLI Now, dear, you mustn't let that woman worry you.

ROSE But she does. She always does. However hard I try not to
mind.

MARTELLI She's getting worse. She didn't use to be so bad.

ROSE One should pity her, I know. Fancy thirty years in a girls'
school. It must have affected her disposition.

MARTELLI And she was principal, too. Everyone deferred to her
then.

ROSE I expect she's lonely. I'm so lucky. I have you for my friend,
and I have Charlie, and now Alison's coming.

MARTELLI Yes, dear, Alison. Isn't it wonderful?

ROSE And *she* hasn't had a visitor for over a year. (*Giggles*) Oh,
how naughty of me. I shouldn't have said that.

(*Enter* NANCY *carrying a florist's box behind her back*)

NANCY Surprise, Mrs. Rose! Look, what's come for you. Flowers!

ROSE Charlie! He never forgets. (*Unwraps box*)

NANCY How exciting. I love flowers.

MARTELLI So do I. Let me smell them. (ROSE *offers box to her*) Mmm.
Delicious. Carnations. What colour are they? (ROSE *is
reading card*) Mrs. Rose?

ROSE (*Unhappily*) They're white. White carnations.

MARTELLI What's wrong?

ROSE Nothing.

NANCY Don't you like white carnations?

ROSE   I'm an ungrateful old woman. Such a good son. Keeps me in every comfort. Never forgets, birthday, Mother's day, Easter. But I would like to see his own handwriting. (*She holds out card*) Look. "With love from Charles." Not even Charlie, mind you. I've never called him Charles in his whole life. I don't believe he sent the flowers at all.

MARTELLI   But of course he did, dear. He must have ordered them.

NANCY   And didn't they come by wire, Mrs. Rose? Then it couldn't be his writing.

ROSE   I suppose you're right.

NANCY   Shall I arrange them for you?

ROSE   Thank you, dear.

NANCY   (*On her way out*) Would you like them in your room?

ROSE   No, bring them back in here. Then Mrs. Martelli can smell them.

MARTELLI   And look at them. (*Smiles*) I can feel their whiteness.

(*As* NANCY *is leaving she meets* FANSHAWE *returning with a book*)

FANSHAWE   What have you got there? The inevitable, I suppose?

NANCY   The inevitable? They're carnations for Mrs. Rose.

FANSHAWE   With monotonous regularity her son sends carnations. I detest the flowers. They remind me of funerals.

NANCY   Well, that's too bad. (*She exits*)

MARTELLI   Yes. Because they remind us of birthdays, Miss Fanshawe. Please remember that.

GIBBS   Yes, birthdays. Tee hee. Seventy-seven. Not funerals. Six dead. Where's seven?

(FANSHAWE *sits at table with a snort of disgust, and picks up her cards.* MATRON *enters*)

MATRON   I have a treat for the birthday girl. Mrs. Rose, I've arranged for you and Alison to have a nice cozy lunch all by yourselves in my private sitting room.

ROSE   Oh, Matron, how good of you.

MATRON   And Cook's made a little birthday cake with seven candles. Alison will like that.

ROSE   Dear Matron, I don't know what I've done to deserve such kindness.

FANSHAWE   Neither do we.

GIBBS   Fanny's jealous. Fanny's jealous.

FANSHAWE   I assure you it is very disagreeable to be obliged to see my former students in my bedroom.

MATRON   But your bedroom's so large, Miss Fanshawe.

FANSHAWE   Nevertheless, at St. Hilda's I always impressed upon my girls, that the one place a lady never entertains is the bedroom.

MARTELLI   I believe times have changed.

MATRON   Well, well, Miss Fanshawe. Let me know the next time you expect visitors, and I'll see what can be done.

GIBBS   Nothing doing, Fanny. Nothing doing.

MATRON   Now, Mrs. Rose, come with me and we'll get you dressed.

ROSE   We'll have the crossword later, Mrs. Martelli.

MARTELLI   That's all right, dear, it won't run away.

(Exit MATRON *pushing* MRS. ROSE*)*

(Feels watch) Miss Gibbs, nearly time for the weather.

GIBBS   *(Chanting)* Weather, feather, leather, heather. Weather, Fanny!

FANSHAWE   This place is past endurance.

MARTELLI   But we have to endure.

FANSHAWE   You're the only intelligent one here. You're the only one I can talk to, and you spend all your time with her.

MARTELLI   Mrs. Rose is my friend. We depend on each other.

FANSHAWE   Everybody needs someone to lean on.

MARTELLI   You're so strong, Miss Fanshawe.

FANSHAWE   Oh I'm strong, all right. I don't need anybody, make no mistake.

(Re-enter NANCY *with the carnations. She puts them down near* MISS FANSHAWE*)*
Don't put them there. I don't want them near me.

*(*NANCY *picks up vase)*

NANCY   But Mrs. Rose asked me to bring them in here.

FANSHAWE   And Fairview Manor is run for the sole benefit of Mrs. Rose?

MARTELLI   Yes, for today it is. (*She gets a small transistor radio out of knitting bag*) Nancy, find another table to put them on. (NANCY *does so*) I can still smell them from here. Now, please take this radio over to Miss Gibbs.

GIBBS   (*Taking radio*) Weather forecast. Most important. Racing this afternoon.

(GIBBS *cackles, turns radio up loud. Announcer's voice booms out: THIS IS THE C.B.C. MARINE WEATHER FORE-CAST, VALID UNTIL THIS TIME TOMORROW. . .*)

FANSHAWE   Bedlam. Sheer bedlam.

MARTELLI   (*Shouting*) Nancy, get her to put the plug in her ear.

(NANCY *helps* GIBBS, *thereby shutting off the noise.* GIBBS *then withdraws, so to speak, from the room*)

NANCY   (*Wide-eyed*) Does she always listen to the weather?

MARTELLI   The marine weather forecast, yes. Every morning at eleven. She told me once, she used to go sailing when she was young. Used to race in English Bay.

NANCY   You're kidding? All that long time ago? You mean there was sailing then, here in Vancouver?

MARTELLI   (*Laughing*) Yes, Nancy.

FANSHAWE   Ridiculous. Now she never sets foot outside the house.

MARTELLI   If the weather forecast gives her pleasure, I don't see why she should be denied it.

FANSHAWE   No one considers my pleasure, or what I want. This place is a bear garden. (*She gets up. Exits*)

MARTELLI   (*Sighs*) Oh dear.

NANCY   She's a real bitch, isn't she?

MARTELLI   We have to be tolerant, Nancy.

NANCY   Sorry. I shouldn't have said that.

MARTELLI   Poor Miss Fanshawe, she's so unhappy, so unresigned.

NANCY   Why does she stay here, then?

MARTELLI   I suppose because she's always lived in an institution, can't manage by herself.

NANCY   Hasn't she any friends?

MARTELLI   I've never heard her mention any, only her old students.

NANCY   I read once that the most difficult people are often the most insecure. Do you think that's true?

MARTELLI   I should think it's quite possible. Now, if you're not busy, my dear, could we wind my wool?

NANCY   Certainly. (NANCY *sits on stool, takes wool in her hands.* MARTELLI *starts to wind*)

MARTELLI   The carnations smell glorious. Remind me of Paris in the spring.

NANCY   I had a carnation corsage once. Years ago when I was a kid in junior high.

MARTELLI   (*Smiles*) Years ago? Did you?

NANCY   Ever since, they've reminded me of dancing. I adore dancing.

MARTELLI   Ah, so did I, once. But alas, those days are gone. Now there's only dignity, security and happiness.

NANCY   Excuse me, but isn't that quite . . . suitable . . . for older people?

MARTELLI   Suitable, it might be, dull it certainly is. Tell me, my dear, why are you working here?

NANCY   I need the money. I looked after my grandmother so I know what to do for old people. They warned me it might get me down. Don't laugh, I know it sounds corny, but I wanted to do something for someone else.

MARTELLI   Ah, Nancy, you're in love.

NANCY   You're amazing, Mrs. Martelli.

MARTELLI   It wasn't very difficult. I suppose you live together?

NANCY   Yes.

MARTELLI   And are very happy.

NANCY   Mrs. Martelli, I expected you to be shocked.

MARTELLI   Shocked? I'm not shocked, I've been young.

NANCY   But weren't things different then? Do you know what it is to love a guy so much it hurts?

MARTELLI   I don't imagine love has changed.

NANCY   (*A small smile*) I'm putting him through college. That's why I need the money.

MARTELLI   What a pity you can't go, too.

NANCY   I did. I was in music, but I quit. Anyway, Kevin's more talented than I am.

MARTELLI   Talented?

NANCY   He writes. He hasn't published anything yet. But I know he will. He puts me in his stories. Altered, you know, but I can recognize myself just the same. If he tells how a girl makes love to Mozart, or shaves her legs in the bath, I know it's me he's talking about.

MARTELLI Well, I never.

NANCY Maybe you wouldn't approve of him, Mrs. Martelli. His hair is long. He puts a rubber band around it when he's typing. It's black and shiny and beautiful. And when he tells me he loves me, don't laugh . . . but I want to sing or cry, I'm so happy.

MARTELLI To sing or cry? I remember feeling like that. I remember singing Schubert for sheer joy. Well, well, my dear. So many years ago. Before the First World War, it was, in Paris.

NANCY How romantic. It sounds like *La Boheme.*

MARTELLI It wasn't a bit like *Boheme*, I can tell you. I was studying at the Conservatoire, working very hard. I practised the piano eight hours a day. That is, until I met Mario. Mario Martelli. He had the practice room next to mine. First I fell in love with his violin, then with him. After that I'm afraid we sadly neglected our music. Italians have a great talent for making love, my dear. It was the most enchanting period of my life.

NANCY When did you marry him, Mrs. Martelli?

MARTELLI Marry him? I didn't marry him. I became pregnant, but he never knew. Oh, we might have married had circumstances been different. As it was, I went away to have the child. It was a boy, stillborn. So all I had left was Mario's name. I took that. It was a comfort to call myself Martelli. A sort of remembrance of things past. When I returned to Canada, I told everyone my husband had died suddenly. For a few years I gave concerts. Later, I taught the piano. The name, Madame Martelli, was quite an asset, so much more impressive than my own. (*Laughs*) I shouldn't be boring you with this ancient history, my dear. You've a very sympathetic listener.

NANCY Have you told the others?

MARTELLI Bless me, no. They wouldn't be interested. If they ever knew what love was, they've forgotten.

NANCY I won't forget.

(MATRON *enters pushing* ROSE, *who has changed into a blue dress*)

MATRON You two seem to be getting along fine.

NANCY   (*Enthusiastic*) Oh we are.

(She gets up, helps settle MRS. ROSE. GIBBS *takes plug out of ear. Shuts off radio)*

MARTELLI   Nancy is a great addition to the staff. It's been a breath of fresh air to talk to someone young.
GIBBS   (*Cackling*) A breath of air. Winds brisk to moderate. Small craft warning.
MATRON   Small craft warning. Very nice. That's nice to know.

*(*GIBBS *cackles,* NANCY *collects radio, returns it to* MARTELLI'S *bag)*

ROSE   A breath of fresh air? Mrs. Martelli, it's a long time since you've been out of Fairview Manor.
MARTELLI   Yes, Mrs. Rose, it has.
ROSE   I've had an inspiration. I'm going to ask Alison if, after lunch, she will drive us down to the band concert. We can park under the trees and you can hear the Pastoral Symphony. Wouldn't that be a treat?
MARTELLI   A treat, indeed. But will she have time?
ROSE   I'm sure Charlie's girl will make time for her old Gran.
NANCY   She certainly should. Especially on your birthday.
MATRON   Well, it would be a nice outing for you ladies, if it can be arranged.
ROSE   (*Looks at watch*) Not much longer to wait. Do I look all right?
MATRON   You always look so pretty in that dress.
NANCY   It matches your eyes, Mrs. Rose.
MARTELLI   Then it must be your blue dress. Now I've been told, I can feel its blueness.

*(*FANSHAWE *enters)*

GIBBS   Ohoh. Storm warning. Fanny's back.
FANSHAWE   (*Furious*) No doubt you would all prefer a total eclipse.

(Silence for a moment)

MATRON   (*Tactfully*) Have you been for your walk, Miss Fanshawe?
FANSHAWE   No, I have not.
ROSE   (*To* MATRON) I thought I'd give Alison this. (*She brings a small box out of her bag*) A little trinket to remember me by.
MATRON   Oh, Mrs. Rose, your favourite brooch. Won't you miss it? Why not leave it to Alison in your will?
ROSE   But I would like to think of her having it now. Do you think she'd like it, Nancy?
NANCY   I'm sure she'd love it.
FANSHAWE   That ugly thing? It's too old-fashioned. She'd never wear it.
NANCY   I think it's beautiful, and old-fashioned jewellry is right in style now.
ROSE   I always thought it was a pretty brooch. My hubby gave it to me when we were first married. I was about your age, my dear. No doubt one of these days someone will give you something you will treasure all your life.
NANCY   (*Smiling*) I hope so.
MATRON   Well, Mrs. Rose, it's yours to do with as you like. But you mustn't get over-excited. Remember your blood pressure. (*Hands her a glass of water and a pill*) Take your pill, please.
MARTELLI   Let's do the crossword, Mrs. Rose.
ROSE   I suppose it will help pass the time.
MATRON   It will take your mind off the time.

(*MATRON removes glass*)

NANCY   And here's the paper in your chair. Ready at the place, too. (*Hands newspaper*)
MATRON   (*Starts out*) Now, everybody had coffee? I'll bring Alison to you, just as soon as she arrives.

(*Exit* MATRON *pushing trolley*)

ROSE   Now, let me see, where are we? Ready, Mrs. Martelli? The first word across is . . .
GIBBS   (*To tune of* Happy Birthday) Happy crossword to you . . . happy crossword to you . . .
MARTELLI   Thank you, Miss Gibbs.

GIBBS   Happy crossword, dear people. No, wrong. Happy birthday,
        dear Rose, happy birthday . . .
ROSE   (*Louder*) The first word has eleven letters.
FANSHAWE   Must you shout? Mrs. Martelli may be blind, but she's
        not deaf.
ROSE   Sorry. Eleven letters: a slow dance on a ground bass theme.
        Oh, how difficult. Is it something to do with music?
MARTELLI   A slow dance on a ground bass theme. (*Counts on
        fingers*) Eleven letters.
NANCY   Oh, what is it? I know it, I know it.
MARTELLI   Bach. One associates it with Bach.
NANCY   That's right. Oh, it's on the tip of my tongue.
MARTELLI   I'll have it in a minute.
GIBBS   Hey, Fanny.
FANSHAWE   Be quiet.
GIBBS   You hear me, Fanny?
MARTELLI   Passacaglia. The answer's Passacaglia.
NANCY   Of course! Passacaglia! Mrs. Martelli you're fantastic.
MARTELLI   Well, I should know it. I used to play them often enough.
ROSE   However do you spell it?
MARTELLI   P–A–S–S–A–

*(The telephone, insistent and penetrating, begins to ring at
five-second intervals, while* GIBBS *chants "Fanny" and*
MARTELLI *spells out the word. The result is indeed
bedlam)*

GIBBS   Hey, Fanny, Fanny, Fanny, Fanny, Fanny . . . (*She goes on*)
NANCY   (*Going to her*) Now, Miss Gibbs. You mustn't be so noisy.
GIBBS   Noisy?
NANCY   Yes. (*Inspired*) Like a fog horn.
GIBBS   (*Imitating sound of fog horn*) Fan–nee. Fan–nee.
NANCY   No, Miss Gibbs. Quiet.
MARTELLI   (*Carrying on during this*) –C–A–G–L–I–A.
ROSE   Oh dear, I've broken the pencil.
NANCY   I have one here, Mrs. Rose. (*Hands one from her pocket*)
GIBBS   Fan–nee. Fan–nee.
FANSHAWE   What's the matter with you, girl. Why don't you answer
        that telephone?
NANCY   (*To* MARTELLI) Do you think I should?
MARTELLI   Yes, dear, you better. It might be important.
GIBBS   Fanny! Count my flies. Got six, Fanny, six dead.

FANSHAWE This is absolutely unendurable. If Matron won't co-operate I shall write to the Board of Directors, myself. Miss Gibbs must be removed. Fairview Manor is not a mental institution. The prospectus offers dignity, security and happiness.

MARTELLI I often think she's the happiest one of the lot of us.

FANSHAWE And what about my dignity? It's always me she attacks. Why should I put with being bawled at by a . . . bakerwoman.

GIBBS Bakerwoman . . . bakerwoman.

MARTELLI She'd stop teasing, if only you'd humour her.

FANSHAWE I shall do nothing of the kind. And what about our visitors? Mrs. Rose's granddaughter, for example, it's disgraceful that she should be exposed to such a person.

MARTELLI Oh, come now.

ROSE Yes, please . . . I'm rather fond of Miss Gibbs. Alison will understand.

FANSHAWE Alison will understand! My dear woman, you haven't the slightest idea what you're talking about; I'm sure your famous daughter-in-law would object to Alison meeting that imbecile.

GIBBS Imbecile, Fanny?

MARTELLI Really, Miss Fanshawe, you go too far.

FANSHAWE If you take my advice, Matron should be asked to see that Miss Gibbs is confined to her room while Alison is here.

MARTELLI That's quite unnecessary.

FANSHAWE Unnecessary? Nonsense!

MARTELLI We all live here together.

ROSE Yes. Please, Miss Fanshawe, it's my birthday and you're upsetting me.

FANSHAWE Oh, so I upset you, do I? It seems I upset everyone at Fairview Manor.

GIBBS Watch out! Barometer falling.

ROSE (Pleading) Please don't let's quarrel when Alison's coming.

FANSHAWE (Ominously) You mean you hope she's coming.

ROSE You know quite well she's coming. I have the telegram.

FANSHAWE Oh, the telegram. Proof positive, of course. You don't . . .

(NANCY enters, visibly distressed)

NANCY (Tentatively) Mrs. Rose?

FANSHAWE   Don't interrupt, please, miss. (*To* ROSE) You don't really believe Alison will actually come, do you? For how many years now have you been blathering about a visit from these precious relatives of yours? But they've never shown up yet, have they?

MARTELLI   Miss Fanshawe, that's enough! What were you saying, Nancy?

(NANCY *gasps and runs from the room*)

ROSE   (*Tearfully*) It's not easy for them to leave. Charlie has an important position.

FANSHAWE   Oh we understand that all right. Important enough to pay a well-trained secretary. Four times a year, always on time, white carnations, with love from Charles.

(ROSE *starts to choke*)

MARTELLI   How dare you! Don't listen to her, dear.

FANSHAWE   Why shouldn't she listen to me? I've listened to her, heaven knows.

(ROSE *is sobbing louder*)

MARTELLI   (*Gets up, gropes for door*) Nancy! Nancy, please come and get Mrs. Rose.

FANSHAWE   Carol and Charlie. Charlie and Carol. Alison, Alison, Alison.

MARTELLI   Stop it at once!

FANSHAWE   Petted and pampered. A birthday cake. Matron's sitting room. We all know the whole thing's a sham.

MARTELLI   We know nothing of the sort. (*She fumbles at* ROSE'S *wheelchair, tries to push her out, but it gets jammed against the furniture*) Nancy, where are you? Fetch Matron!

FANSHAWE   Oh yes, fetch Matron, you can count on her. But the fact remains that the only time this precious Charlie ever thinks of his mother, is when he looks in his cheque book and sees what it costs him to keep her there.

MARTELLI   You wicked, wicked, woman.

(ROSE *has been sobbing hysterically. Now she gives a great shuddering gasp and collapses.* MATRON *and* NANCY *rush in*)

NANCY   (*Distraught, as they enter*) I couldn't tell her, Matron, I just couldn't.

(MATRON *goes to* ROSE, *feels her pulse*)

MATRON   Phone the doctor to come at once, Nancy.
MARTELLI   Dear God.
MATRON   His number's on my desk.

(NANCY *runs out*)

FANSHAWE   Another one of her attacks. She was over-excited. We could all see she was working up to it.

(MATRON *starts to push* ROSE *out*)

MARTELLI   Matron, is she . . .
MATRON   I'm taking her to her room. There's nothing you can do.

(MARTELLI *returns to her chair. Exit* MATRON *with* ROSE)

MARTELLI   (*Very quietly, to* FANSHAWE) Well, are you satisfied?
FANSHAWE   I don't know what you mean.
MARTELLI   She lived for her family. They were everything to her.
FANSHAWE   We all have to face old age, neglect.
MARTELLI   If she dies, you'll have killed her.
GIBBS   Another one dead! Seven dead!
FANSHAWE   (*Screaming*) Shut up. (*To* MARTELLI) What do you know about it? You're blind. You can't see.

MARTELLI   I have indeed been blind, and I'm deeply sorry. Even so, it was cruel, not worthy of you.

FANSHAWE   (*Breaking*) What if it was? You're all against me. I've had enough. Enough of the whole lot of you. Understand? Enough. (*She bursts into tears and stumbles out*)

GIBBS   (*Moved*) Rain today. Rain tomorrow. Poor Fanny, Fanny's crying.

(Silence for a moment. NANCY *enters slowly)*

NANCY   Oh, Mrs. Martelli, how awful it all is.

MARTELLI   Old age is awful.

NANCY   (*Near tears*) That telephone call . . .

MARTELLI   Yes?

NANCY   . . . was from Alison. (*In a rush*) She's not coming. She met some friends on the plane. How could she, Mrs. Martelli, how *could* she?

MARTELLI   Is that all?

NANCY   She said she'd try and drop in on her way home next month. I was so disgusted, I hung up. (*Painfully*) And then . . . I came back in here to tell Mrs. Rose . . . and I couldn't do it . . . If I had, do you think things would have been different?

MARTELLI   No, dear, you mustn't blame yourself. In many ways I feel responsible for what has happened.

NANCY   You?

MARTELLI   I should have seen what was going on. We're all vulnerable, no matter what we might say to the contrary.

NANCY   Do you think Mrs. Rose will die?

MARTELLI   I don't know. She's had these attacks before. But this time . . . I must admit, I hope she will not recover.

NANCY   Mrs. Martelli! What a terrible thing to say!

MARTELLI   Is it Nancy? After what's happened today?

NANCY   Poor, poor Mrs. Rose.

MARTELLI   Yes. Poor Mrs. Rose. Poor Miss Fanshawe.

NANCY   Poor Miss Fanshawe?

MARTELLI   Lonely and unloved. (*Pause*) Nancy, you're too young to work here.

GIBBS   Seven dead. I'm hungry. Lunch time?

MARTELLI   Yes, Miss Gibbs. Lunch time.

NANCY   Is it only lunch time?

MARTELLI   Yes, my dear. I told you eight hours is a long day.

(NANCY *gives* MRS. MARTELLI *her arm. Slowly they walk out, as the lights fade, lingering momentarily on the carnations)*

After the Play Suggestions:

For Writing and Discussion

1. Fairview Manor offers "Dignity, Security and Happiness." Are the owners of the home misleading the residents? Explain.
2. Make a list of the names of retirement homes in your area and describe the mental pictures that these names create for you. What do these "pictures" tell us about the way that we look at senior citizens?
3. Why does Fanshawe treat Mrs. Rose in such a horrible way? Is she simply a mean person, or can another explanation be given for her actions?
4. What makes Mrs. Martelli so content with her lot in life?
5. Why did the playwright put Mrs. Gibbs in the play?
6. Do you think Mrs. Rose suspects that her granddaughter will not come?
7. What draws Nancy and Mrs. Martelli together?
8. A playwright must prepare an audience for what eventually happens in the play. A completely unexpected outcome usually has little effect on an audience, except perhaps to make them laugh. In what ways does Joan Hurley "prepare" us for (a) Mrs. Rose's attack? (b) the granddaughter's telephone call?
9. Mrs. Martelli tells Nancy that Mrs. Gibbs used to sail on English Bay. Nancy is surprised. Why?
10. The play, *Passacaglia*, has as its subtitle, "a slow dance on a ground bass theme." In what way is life in the retirement home a "slow dance"?
11. At the end of the play Nancy asks, "Is it only lunch time?". Discuss.
12. If you were the set designer of *Passacaglia*, what would you do to make the living room of Fairview Manor reflect the feeling of the title and subtitle?

For Presentation

If your school or board of education has video-taping equipment, this would be a good place to try using it. Divide the script among the members of the class as for the other plays, leaving a small group to do the production work. Each group should do a "storyboard" or cartoon strip of the key moments in their scene, showing the camera operator each new shot or picture. In your production group you will need a director, camera operator and one or two properties people. The director (or teacher) can make sure that all the groups have rehearsed their scenes and prepared their storyboards before the actual taping begins. He or she will also arrange the groups for the actual taping and, using the storyboards, direct the camera operator. The camera person should be well practised on the equipment before the day of the actual shooting. The best method of preparation would be to film the groups as they are rehearsing. The properties people will locate the necessary "hand props" (the things the actors actually use such as cards, glasses, etc.) and find as many realistic items for the set as they can.

Hints:

(a) Think carefully about the people you saw in the "senior citizens" home. Try to make your portrayals as real as possible.
(b) What action is there? How do the old people spend their time? Read the script *carefully* for details.

Augustus Does His Bit

by George Bernard Shaw

Augustus Does His Bit was first performed at the Royal Court Theatre in London, England, by the Stage Society, on January 21, 1917.

George Bernard Shaw was born in Ireland in 1856 and died in England in 1950. One of the foremost dramatists of the English stage, he was also a novelist, critic, essayist and social reformer. Most of his plays are still performed regularly. The Shaw Festival at Niagara-on-the-Lake, Ontario was established mainly for the presentation of his work.

George Bernard Shaw

Before the Play

Go to the library and read about World War I; find out what happened during the year 1916. Using this information, and working in pairs, improvise a conversation between a well-informed coward and a conceited recruiting officer. The job of the recruiting officer is to get the coward's signature on a registration form. When you have done that, try switching roles. There is no need to perform this improvisation for the class; it can be done at your seats with your partner.

The Mayor's parlor in the Town Hall of Little Pifflington. Lord Augustus Highcastle, a distinguished member of the governing class, in the uniform of a colonel, and very well preserved at forty-five, is comfortably seated at a writing table with his heels on it, reading The Morning Post. The door faces him, a little to his left, at the other side of the room. The window is behind him. In the fireplace, a gas stove. On the table a bell button and a telephone. Portraits of past Mayors, in robes and gold chains, adorn the walls. An elderly clerk with a short white beard and whiskers, and a very red nose, shuffles in.

AUGUSTUS *(Hastily putting aside his paper and replacing his feet on the floor)* Hullo! Who are you?

THE CLERK   The staff (*a slight impediment in his speech adds to the impression of incompetence produced by his age and appearance*).

AUGUSTUS   You the staff! What do you mean, man?

THE CLERK   What I say. There aint anybody else.

AUGUSTUS   Tush! Where are the others?

THE CLERK   At the front.

AUGUSTUS   Quite right. Most proper. Why arnt you at the front?

THE CLERK   Over age. Fifty-seven.

AUGUSTUS   But you can still do your bit. Many an older man is in the G.R.'s, or volunteering for home defence.

THE CLERK   I have volunteered.

AUGUSTUS   Then why are you not in uniform?

THE CLERK   They said they wouldn't have me if I was given away
with a pound of tea. Told me to go home and not be an old
silly. (*A sense of unbearable wrong, til now only smoulder-
ing in him, bursts into flame*) Young Bill Knight, that I took
with me, got two and sevenpence. I got nothing. Is it justice?
This country is going to the dogs, if you ask me.

AUGUSTUS   (*Rising indignantly*) I do not ask you, sir; I will not allow
you to say such things in my presence. Our statesmen are
the greatest known to history. Our generals are invincible.
Our army is the admiration of the world. (*Furiously*) How
dare you tell me that the country is going to the dogs!

THE CLERK   Why did they give young Bill Knight two and
sevenpence, and not give me even my tram fare? Do you
call that being great statesmen? As good as robbing me, I
call it.

AUGUSTUS   Thats enough. Leave the room. (*He sits down and takes
up his pen, settling himself to work.* THE CLERK *shuffles to the
door.* AUGUSTUS *adds, with cold politeness*) Send me the
Secretary.

THE CLERK   I'm the Secretary. I cant leave the room and send myself
to you at the same time, can I?

AUGUSTUS   Dont be insolent. Where is the gentleman I have been
corresponding with: Mr. Horatio Floyd Beamish?

THE CLERK   (*Returning and bowing*) Here. Me.

AUGUSTUS   You! Ridiculous. What right have you to call yourself
by a pretentious name of that sort?

THE CLERK   You may drop the Horatio Floyd. Beamish is good
enough for me.

AUGUSTUS   Is there nobody else to take my instructions?

THE CLERK   It's me or nobody. And for two pins I'd chuck it. Dont
you drive me too far. Old uns like me is up in the world
now.

AUGUSTUS   If we were not at war, I should discharge you on the
spot for disrespectful behavior. But England is in danger;
and I cannot think of my personal dignity at such a moment.
(*Shouting at him*) Dont you think of yours, either, worm that
you are; or I'll have you arrested under the Defence of the
Realm Act, double quick.

THE CLERK   What do I care about the realm? They done me out of
two and seven—

AUGUSTUS   Oh, damn your two and seven! Did you receive my
letters?

THE CLERK   Yes.

AUGUSTUS   I addressed a meeting here last night — went straight to the platform from the train. I wrote to you that I should expect you to be present and report yourself. Why did you not do so?

THE CLERK   The police wouldnt let me on the platform.

AUGUSTUS   Did you tell them who you were?

THE CLERK   They knew who I was. Thats why they wouldnt let me up.

AUGUSTUS   This is too silly for anything. This town wants waking up. I made the best recruiting speech I ever made in my life; and not a man joined.

THE CLERK   What did you expect? You told them our gallant fellows is falling at the rate of a thousand a day in the big push. Dying for Little Pifflington, you says. Come and take their places, you says. That aint the way to recruit.

AUGUSTUS   But I expressly told them their widows would have pensions.

THE CLERK   I heard you. Would have been all right if it had been the widows you wanted to get round.

AUGUSTUS   (Rising angrily) This town is inhabited by dastards. I say it with a full sense of responsibility, dastards! They call themselves Englishmen; and they are afraid to fight.

THE CLERK   Afraid to fight! You should see them on a Saturday night.

AUGUSTUS   Yes: they fight one another; but they wont fight the Germans.

THE CLERK   They got grudges again one another: how can they have grudges again the Huns that they never saw? Theyve no imagination: thats what it is. Bring the Huns here; and theyll quarrel with them fast enough.

AUGUSTUS   (Returning to his seat with a grunt of disgust) Mf! Theyll have them here if theyre not careful. (Seated) Have you carried out my orders about the war saving?

THE CLERK   Yes.

AUGUSTUS   The allowance of petrol has been reduced by three quarters?

THE CLERK   It has.

AUGUSTUS   And you have told the motor-car people to come here and arrange to start munition work now that their motor business is stopped?

THE CLERK   It aint stopped. Theyre busier than ever.

AUGUSTUS   Busy at what?

THE CLERK   Making small cars.

AUGUSTUS   New cars!

THE CLERK   The old cars only do twelve miles to the gallon. Everybody has to have a car that will do thirty-five now.

AUGUSTUS   Cant they take the train?

THE CLERK   There aint no trains now. Theyve tore up the rails and sent them to the front.

AUGUSTUS   Psha!

THE CLERK   Well, we have to get about somehow.

AUGUSTUS   This is perfectly monstrous. Not in the least what I intended.

THE CLERK   Hell—

AUGUSTUS   Sir!

THE CLERK   (*Explaining*) Hell, they says, is paved with good intentions.

AUGUSTUS   (*Springing to his feet*) Do you mean to insinuate that hell is paved with my good intentions — with the good intentions of His Majesty's Government?

THE CLERK   I dont mean to insinuate anything until the Defence of the Realm Act is repealed. It aint safe.

AUGUSTUS   They told me that this town had set an example to all England in the matter of economy. I came down here to promise the Mayor a knighthood for his exertions.

THE CLERK   The Mayor! Where do *I* come in?

AUGUSTUS   You dont come in. You go out. This is a fool of a place. I'm greatly disappointed. Deeply disappointed. (*Flinging himself back into his chair*) Disgusted.

THE CLERK   What more can we do? Weve shut up everything. The picture gallery is shut. The museum is shut. The theatres and picture shows is shut: I havnt seen a movy picture for six months.

AUGUSTUS   Man, man: do you want to see picture shows when the Hun is at the gate?

THE CLERK   (*Mournfully*) I dont now, though it drove me melancholy mad at first. I was on the point of taking a pennorth of rat poison—

AUGUSTUS   Why didnt you?

THE CLERK   Because a friend advised me to take a drink instead. That saved my life, though it makes me very poor company in the mornings, as (*Hiccuping*) perhaps youve noticed.

AUGUSTUS   Well, upon my soul! You are not ashamed to stand there and confess yourself a disgusting drunkard.

THE CLERK   Well, what of it? We're at war now; and everything's changed. Besides, I should lose my job here if I stood drinking at the bar. I'm a respectable man and must buy my

111

drink and take it home with me. And they wont serve me with less than a quart. If youd told me before the war that I could get through a quart of whisky in a day, I shouldnt have believed you. Thats the good of war: it brings out powers in a man that he never suspected himself capable of. You said so yourself in your speech last night.

AUGUSTUS   I did not know that I was talking to an imbecile. You ought to be ashamed of yourself. There must be an end of this drunken slacking. I'm going to establish a new order of things here. I shall come down every morning before breakfast until things are properly in train. Have a cup of coffee and two rolls for me here every morning at half-past ten.

THE CLERK   You cant have no rolls. The only baker that baked rolls was a Hun; and he's been interned.

AUGUSTUS   Quite right, too. And was there no Englishman to take his place?

THE CLERK   There was. But he was caught spying; and they took him up to London and shot him.

AUGUSTUS   Shot an Englishman!

THE CLERK   Well, it stands to reason if the Germans wanted a spy they wouldnt employ a German that everybody would suspect, dont it?

AUGUSTUS   (*Rising again*) Do you mean to say, you scoundrel, that an Englishman is capable of selling his country to the enemy for gold?

THE CLERK   Not as a general thing I wouldnt say it; but theres men here would sell their own mothers for two coppers if they got the chance.

AUGUSTUS   Beamish: it's an ill bird that fouls its own nest.

THE CLERK   It wasnt me that let Little Pifflington get foul. *I* dont belong to the governing classes. I only tell you why you cant have no rolls.

AUGUSTUS   (*Intensely irritated*) Can you tell me where I can find an intelligent being to take my orders?

THE CLERK   One of the street sweepers used to teach in the school until it was shut up for the sake of economy. Will he do?

AUGUSTUS   What! You mean to tell me that when the lives of the gallant fellows in our trenches, and the fate of the British Empire, depend on our keeping up the supply of shells, you are wasting money on sweeping the streets?

THE CLERK   We have to. We dropped it for a while; but the infant death rate went up something frightful.

AUGUSTUS   What matters the death rate of Little Pifflington in a moment like this? Think of our gallant soldiers, not of your squalling infants.

THE CLERK   If you want soldiers you must have children. You cant buy em in boxes, like toy soldiers.

AUGUSTUS   Beamish: the long and the short of it is, you are no patriot. Go downstairs to your office; and have that gas stove taken away and replaced by an ordinary grate. The Board of Trade has urged on me the necessity for economizing gas.

THE CLERK   Our orders from the Minister of Munitions is to use gas instead of coal, because it saves material. Which is it to be?

AUGUSTUS   (*Bawling furiously at him*) Both! Dont criticize your orders: obey them. Yours not to reason why: yours but to do and die. Thats war. (*Cooling down*) Have you anything else to say?

THE CLERK   Yes: I want a rise.

AUGUSTUS   (*Reeling against the table in his horror*) A rise! Horatio Floyd Beamish: do you know that we are at war?

THE CLERK   (*Feebly ironical*) I have noticed something about it in the papers. Heard you mention it once or twice, now I come to think of it.

AUGUSTUS   Our gallant fellows are dying in the trenches; and you want a rise!

THE CLERK   What are they dying for? To keep me alive, aint it? Well, whats the good of that if I'm dead of hunger by the time they come back?

AUGUSTUS   Everybody else is making sacrifices without a thought of self; and you —

THE CLERK   Not half, they aint. Wheres the baker's sacrifice? Wheres the coal merchant's? Wheres the butcher's? Charging me double: thats how they sacrifice themselves. Well, I want to sacrifice myself that way too. Just double next Saturday: double and not a penny less; or no secretary for you (*He stiffens himself shakily, and makes resolutely for the door*).

AUGUSTUS   (*Looking after him contemptuously*) Go: miserable pro-German.

THE CLERK   (*Rushing back and facing him*) Who are you calling a pro-German?

AUGUSTUS   Another word, and I charge you under the Act with discouraging me. Go.

(THE CLERK *blenches and goes out, cowed*)
(*The telephone rings*)

113

AUGUSTUS   (*Taking up the telephone receiver*) Hallo . . . Yes: who
          are you? . . . oh, Blueloo, is it? . . . Yes: theres nobody in the
          room: fire away . . . What? . . . A spy! . . . A woman! . . .
          Yes: I brought it down with me. Do you suppose I'm such a
          fool as to let it out of my hands? Why, it gives a list of all our
          anti-aircraft emplacements from Ramsgate to Skegness. The
          Germans would give a million for it — what? . . . But how
          could she possibly know about it? I havnt mentioned it to a
          soul, except, of course, dear Lucy. . . . Oh, Toto and Lady
          Popham and that lot: they dont count: theyre all right. I
          mean that I havnt mentioned it to any Germans. . . . Pooh!
          Dont you be nervous, old chap. I know you think me a fool:
          but I'm not such a fool as all that. If she tries to get it out of
          me I'll have her in the Tower before you ring up again. (*The
          clerk returns*) Sh-sh! Somebody's just come in: ring off.
          Goodbye. (*He hangs up the receiver*)
THE CLERK   Are you engaged? (*His manner is strangely softened*)
AUGUSTUS   What business is that of yours? However, if you will
          take the trouble to read the society papers for this week, you
          will see that I am engaged to the Honorable Lucy Popham,
          youngest daughter of—
THE CLERK   That aint what I mean. Can you see a female?
AUGUSTUS   Of course I can see a female as easily as a male. Do you
          suppose I'm blind?
THE CLERK   You dont seem to follow me, somehow. Theres a female
          downstairs: what you might call a lady. She wants to know
          can you see her if I let her up.
AUGUSTUS   Oh, you mean am I disengaged. Tell the lady I have just
          received news of the greatest importance which will occupy
          my entire attention for the rest of the day, and that she must
          write for an appointment.
THE CLERK   I'll ask her to explain her business to me. *I* aint above
          talking to a handsome young female when I get the chance
          (*going*).
AUGUSTUS   Stop. Does she seem to be a person of consequence?
THE CLERK   A regular marchioness, if you ask me.
AUGUSTUS   Hm! Beautiful, did you say?
THE CLERK   A human chrysanthemum, sir, believe me.
AUGUSTUS   It will be extremely inconvenient for me to see her; but
          the country is in danger; and we must not consider our own
          comfort. Think how our gallant fellows are suffering in the
          trenches! Shew her up. (*The clerk makes for the door,
          whistling the latest popular love ballad*) Stop whistling
          instantly, sir. This is not a casino.

THE CLERK   Aint it? You just wait til you see her. (*He goes out*)

(AUGUSTUS *produces a mirror, a comb, and a pot of moustache pomade from the drawer of the writing-table, and sits down before the mirror to put some touches to his toilet.*

(THE CLERK *returns, devotedly ushering a very attractive lady, brilliantly dressed. She has a dainty wallet hanging from her wrist.* AUGUSTUS *hastily covers up his toilet apparatus with The Morning Post, and rises in an attitude of pompous condescension*)

THE CLERK   (*To* AUGUSTUS) Here she is. (*To* THE LADY) May I offer you a chair, lady? (*He places a chair at the writing-table opposite* AUGUSTUS, *and steals out on tiptoe*)
AUGUSTUS   Be seated, madam.
THE LADY   (*Sitting down*) Are you Lord Augustus Highcastle?
AUGUSTUS   (*Sitting also*) Madam: I am.
THE LADY   (*With awe*) The great Lord Augustus?
AUGUSTUS   I should not dream of describing myself so, madam; but no doubt I have impressed my countrymen — and (*bowing gallantly*) may I say my countrywomen — as having some exceptional claims to their consideration.
THE LADY   (*Emotionally*) What a beautiful voice you have!
AUGUSTUS   What you hear, madam, is the voice of my country, which now takes a sweet and noble tone even in the harsh mouth of high officialism.
THE LADY   Please go on. You express yourself so wonderfully.
AUGUSTUS   It would be strange indeed if, after sitting on thirty-seven Royal Commissions, mostly as chairman, I had not mastered the art of public expression. Even the Radical papers have paid me the high compliment of declaring that I am never more impressive than when I have nothing to say.
THE LADY   I never read the Radical papers. All I can tell you is that what we women admire in you is not the politician, but the man of action, the heroic warrior, the *beau sabreur.*
AUGUSTUS   (*Gloomily*) Madam, I beg! Please! My military exploits are not a pleasant subject, unhappily.
THE LADY   Oh, I know, I know. How shamefully you have been treated! What ingratitude! But the country is with you. The

115

women are with you. Oh, do you think all our hearts did not throb and all our nerves thrill when we heard how, when you were ordered to occupy that terrible quarry in Hulluch, and you swept into it at the head of your men like a sea-god riding on a tidal wave, you suddenly sprang over the top shouting 'To Berlin! Forward!'; dashed at the German army single-handed; and were cut off and made prisoner by the Huns?

AUGUSTUS   Yes, madam; and what was my reward? They said I had disobeyed orders, and sent me home. Have they forgotten Nelson in the Baltic? Has any British battle ever been won except by a bold individual initiative? I say nothing of professional jealousy: it exists in the army as elsewhere; but it is a bitter thought to me that the recognition denied me by my own country — or rather by the Radical cabal in the Cabinet which pursues my family with rancorous class hatred — that this recognition, I say, came to me at the hands of an enemy — of a rank Prussian.

THE LADY   You dont say so!

AUGUSTUS   How else should I be here instead of starving to death in Ruhleben? Yes, madam: the Colonel of the Pomeranian regiment which captured me, after learning what I had done, and conversing for an hour with me on European politics and military strategy, declared that nothing would induce him to deprive my country of my services, and set me free. I offered, of course, to procure the release in exchange of a German officer of equal quality; but he would not hear of it. He was kind enough to say he could not believe that a German officer answering to that description existed. (*With emotion*) I had my first taste of the ingratitude of my own country as I made my way back to our lines. A shot from our front trench struck me in the head. I still carry the flattened projectile as a trophy (*He throws it on the table: the noise it makes testifies to its weight*) Had it penetrated to the brain I might never have sat on another Royal Commission. Fortunately we have strong heads, we Highcastles. Nothing has ever penetrated to our brains.

THE LADY   How thrilling! How simple! And how tragic! But you will forgive England? Remember: England! Forgive her.

AUGUSTUS   (*With gloomy magnanimity*) It will make no difference whatever to my services to my country. Though she slay me, yet will I, if not exactly trust in her, at least take my part in her government. I am ever at my country's call. Whether it be the embassy in a leading European capital, a governor-generalship in the tropics, or my humble mission here to make Little Pifflington do its bit, I am always ready for the sacrifice. Whilst England remains England, wherever there is a public job to be done you will find a Highcastle sticking to it. And now, madam, enough of my tragic personal history. You have called on business. What can I do for you?

THE LADY   You have relatives at the Foreign Office, have you not?

AUGUSTUS   (*Haughtily*) Madam: the Foreign Office is staffed by my relatives exclusively.

THE LADY   Has the Foreign Office warned you that you are being pursued by a female spy who is determined to obtain possession of a certain list of gun emplacements —

AUGUSTUS   (*Interrupting her somewhat loftily*) All that is perfectly well known to this department, madam.

THE LADY   (*Surprised and rather indignant*) Is it? Who told you? Was it one of your German brothers-in-law?

AUGUSTUS   (*Injured, remonstrating*) I have only three German brothers-in-law, madam. Really, from your tone, one would suppose that I had several. Pardon my sensitiveness on that subject; but reports are continually being circulated that I have been shot as a traitor in the courtyard of the Ritz Hotel simply because I have German brothers-in-law. (*With feeling*) If you had a German brother-in-law, madam, you would know that nothing else in the world produces so strong an anti-German feeling. Life affords no keener pleasure than finding a brother-in-law's name in the German casualty list.

THE LADY   Nobody knows that better than I. Wait until you hear what I have come to tell you: you will understand me as no one else could. Listen. This spy, this woman—

AUGUSTUS   (*All attention*) Yes?

THE LADY   She is a German. A Hun.

AUGUSTUS   Yes, yes. She would be. Continue.

THE LADY   She is my sister-in-law.

AUGUSTUS   (*Deferentially*) I see you are well connected, madam. Proceed.

THE LADY   Need I add that she is my bitterest enemy?

AUGUSTUS   May I — (*He proffers his hand. They shake, fervently. From this moment onward* AUGUSTUS *becomes more and more confidential, gallant and charming*)

THE LADY   Quite so. Well, she is an intimate friend of your brother at the War Office, Hungerford Highcastle: Blueloo as you call him: I dont know why.

AUGUSTUS   (*Explaining*) He was originally called The Singing

Oyster, because he sang drawing-room ballads with such an extraordinary absence of expression. He was then called the Blue Point for a season or two. Finally he became Blueloo.

THE LADY Oh, indeed: I didnt know. Well, Blueloo is simply infatuated with my sister-in-law; and he has rashly let out to her that this list is in your possession. He forgot himself because he was in a towering rage at its being entrusted to you: his language was terrible. He ordered all the guns to be shifted at once.

AUGUSTUS What on earth did he do that for?

THE LADY I cant imagine. But this I know. She made a bet with him that she would come down here and obtain possession of that list and get clean away into the street with it. He took the bet on condition that she brought it straight back to him at the War Office.

AUGUSTUS Good heavens! And you mean to tell me that Blueloo was such a dolt as to believe that she could succeed? Does he take me for a fool!

THE LADY Oh, impossible! He is jealous of your intellect. The bet is an insult to you: dont you feel that? After what you have done for our country—

AUGUSTUS Oh, never mind that. It is the idiocy of the thing I look at. He'll lose his bet; and serve him right!

THE LADY You feel sure you will be able to resist the siren? I warn you, she is very fascinating.

AUGUSTUS You need have no fear, madam. I hope she will come and try it on. Fascination is a game that two can play at. For centuries the younger sons of the Highcastles have had nothing to do but fascinate attractive females when they were not sitting on Royal Commissions or on duty at Knightsbridge barracks. By Gad, madam, if the siren comes here she will meet her match.

THE LADY I feel that. But if she fails to seduce you—

AUGUSTUS (Blushing) Madam!

THE LADY (Continuing) — from your allegiance—

AUGUSTUS Oh, that!

THE LADY — she will resort to fraud, to force, to anything. She will burgle your office: she will have you attacked and garotted at night in the street.

AUGUSTUS Pooh! I'm not afraid.

THE LADY Oh, your courage will only tempt you into danger. She may get the list after all. It is true that the guns are moved. But she would win her bet.

AUGUSTUS   (*Cautiously*) You did not say that the guns were moved. You said that Blueloo had ordered them to be moved.

THE LADY   Well, that is the same thing, isnt it?

AUGUSTUS   Not quite — at the War Office. No doubt those guns will be moved: possibly even before the end of the war.

THE LADY   Then you think they are there still! But if the German War Office gets the list — and she will copy it before she gives it back to Blueloo, you may depend on it — all is lost.

AUGUSTUS   (*Lazily*) Well, I should not go as far as that. (*Lowering his voice*) Will you swear to me not to repeat what I am going to say to you; for if the British public knew that I had said it, I should be at once hounded down as a pro-German.

THE LADY   I will be silent as the grave. I swear it.

AUGUSTUS   (*Again taking it easily*) Well, our people have for some reason made up their minds that the German War Office is everything that our War Office is not — that it carries promptitude, efficiency, and organization to a pitch of completeness and perfection that must be, in my opinion, destructive to the happiness of the staff. My own view — which you are pledged, remember, not to betray — is that the German War Office is no better than any other War Office. I found that opinion on my observation of the characters of my brothers-in-law: one of whom, by the way, is on the German general staff. I am not at all sure that this list of gun emplacements would receive the smallest attention. You see, there are always so many more important things to be attended to. Family matters, and so on, you understand.

THE LADY   Still, if a question were asked in the House of Commons—

AUGUSTUS   The great advantage of being at war, madam, is that nobody takes the slightest notice of the House of Commons. No doubt it is sometimes necessary for a Minister to soothe the more seditious members of that assembly by giving a pledge or two; but the War Office takes no notice of such things.

THE LADY   (*Staring at him*) Then you think this list of gun emplacements doesnt matter!!

AUGUSTUS   By no means, madam. It matters very much indeed. If this spy were to obtain possession of the list, Blueloo would tell the story at every dinner-table in London; and—

THE LADY   And you might lose your post. Of course.

AUGUSTUS   (*Amazed and indignant*) *I* lose my post! What are you

119

dreaming about, madam? How could I possibly be spared? There are hardly Highcastles enough at present to fill half the posts created by this war. No: Blueloo would not go that far. He is at least a gentleman. But I should be chaffed; and, frankly, I dont like being chaffed.

THE LADY   Of course not. Who does? It would never do. Oh never, never.

AUGUSTUS   I'm glad you see it in that light. And now, as a measure of security, I shall put that list in my pocket. (*He begins searching vainly from drawer to drawer in the writing-table*) Where on earth — ? What the dickens did I — ? Thats very odd: I — Where the deuce — ? I thought I had put it in the — Oh, here it is! No: this is Lucy's last letter.

THE LADY   (*Elegiacally*) Lucy's Last Letter! What a title for a picture play!

AUGUSTUS   (*Delighted*) Yes: it is, isnt it? Lucy appeals to the imagination like no other woman. By the way (*Handing over the letter*) I wonder could you read it for me? Lucy is a darling girl; but I really cant read her writing. In London I get the office typist to decipher it and make me a typed copy; but here there is nobody.

THE LADY   (*Puzzling over it*) It is really almost illegible. I think the beginning is meant for 'Dearest Gus'.

AUGUSTUS   (*Eagerly*) Yes: that is what she usually calls me. Please go on.

THE LADY   (*Trying to decipher it*) "What a" — "what a" — oh yes: "what a forgetful old" — something — "you are!" I cant make out the word.

AUGUSTUS   (*Greatly interested*) Is it blighter? That is a favorite expression of hers.

THE LADY   I think so. At all events it begins with a B. (*Reading*) 'What a forgetful old' — (*She is interrupted by a knock at the door*)

AUGUSTUS   (*Impatiently*) Come in. (THE CLERK *enters, clean shaven and in khaki, with an official paper and an envelope in his hand*) What is this ridiculous mummery, sir?

THE CLERK   (*Coming to the table and exhibiting his uniform to both*) Theyve passed me. The recruiting officer come for me. Ive had my two and seven.

AUGUSTUS   (*Rising wrathfully*) I shall not permit it. What do they mean by taking my office staff? Good God! they will be taking our hunt servants next. (*Confronting* THE CLERK) What did the man mean? What did he say?

THE CLERK   He said that now you was on the job we'd want another million men, and he was going to take the old-age pensioners or anyone he could get.

AUGUSTUS   And did you dare knock at my door and interrupt my business with this lady to repeat this man's ineptitudes?

THE CLERK   No. I come because the waiter from the hotel brought this paper. You left it on the coffee-room breakfast-table this morning.

THE LADY   (*Intercepting it*) It is the list. Good heavens!

THE CLERK   (*Proffering the envelope*) He says he thinks this is the envelope belonging to it.

THE LADY   (*Snatching the envelope also*) Yes! Addressed to you. Lord Augustus! (AUGUSTUS *comes back to the table to look at it*) Oh, how imprudent! Everybody would guess its importance with your name on it. Fortunately I have some letters of my own here (*Opening her wallet*) Why not hide it in one of my envelopes? then no one will dream that the enclosure is of any political value. (*Taking out a letter, she crosses the room towards the window, whispering to* AUGUSTUS *as she passes him*) Get rid of that man.

AUGUSTUS   (*Naughtily approaching* THE CLERK, *who humorously makes a paralytic attempt to stand at attention*) Have you any further business here, pray?

THE CLERK   Am I to give the waiter anything; or will you do it yourself?

AUGUSTUS   Which waiter is it? The English one?

THE CLERK   No: the one that calls hisself a Swiss. Shouldnt wonder if he'd made a copy of that paper.

AUGUSTUS   Keep your impertinent surmises to yourself, sir. Remember that you are in the army now; and let me have no more of your civilian insubordination. Attention! Left turn! Quick march!

THE CLERK   (*Stolidly*) I dunno what you mean.

AUGUSTUS   Go to the guard-room and report yourself for disobeying orders. Now do you know what I mean?

THE CLERK   Now look here. I aint going to argue with you—

AUGUSTUS   Nor I with you. Out with you.

(*He seizes* THE CLERK, *and rushes him through the door. The moment* THE LADY *is left alone, she snatches a sheet of official paper from the stationery rack; folds it so that it resembles the list; compares the two to see that they look exactly alike; whips the list into her wallet; and substitutes the fascimile for it. Then she listens for the return of* AUGUSTUS. *A crash is heard, as of* THE CLERK *falling downstairs)*

(AUGUSTUS *returns and is about to close the door when the voice of* THE CLERK *is heard from below:*

THE CLERK   I'll have the law of you for this, I will.

AUGUSTUS   *(Shouting down to him)* Theres no more law for you, you scoundrel. Youre a soldier now. *(He shuts the door and comes to* THE LADY) Thank heaven, the war has given us the upper hand of these fellows at last. Excuse my violence; but discipline is absolutely necessary in dealing with the lower middle classes.

THE LADY   Serve the insolent creature right! Look! I have found you a beautiful envelope for the list, an unmistakeable lady's envelope. *(She puts the sham list into her envelope and hands it to him)*

AUGUSTUS   Excellent. Really very clever of you. *(Slyly)* Come: would you like to have a peep at the list *(Beginning to take the blank paper from the envelope)*?

THE LADY   *(On the brink of detection)* No no. Oh, please, no.

AUGUSTUS   Why? It wont bite you *(Drawing it out further)*.

THE LADY   *(Snatching at his hand)* Stop. Remember: if there should be an inquiry, you must be able to swear that you never shewed that list to a mortal soul.

AUGUSTUS   Oh, that is a mere form. If you are really curious—

THE LADY   I am not. I couldnt bear to look at it. One of my dearest friends was blown to pieces by an aircraft gun; and since then I have never been able to think of one without horror.

AUGUSTUS   You mean it was a real gun, and actually went off. How sad! how sad! *(He pushes the sham list back into the envelope, and pockets it)*

THE LADY   *(Great sigh of relief)* And now, Lord Augustus, I have taken up too much of your valuable time. Goodbye.

AUGUSTUS   What! Must you go?

THE LADY   You are so busy.

AUGUSTUS   Yes; but not before lunch, you know. I never can do much before lunch. And I'm no good at all in the afternoon. From five to six is my real working time. Must you really go?

THE LADY   I must, really. I have done my business very satisfactor-ily. Thank you ever so much *(She proffers her hand)*.

AUGUSTUS   (*Shaking it affectionately as he leads her to the door, but first pressing the bell button with his left hand*) Goodbye. Goodbye. So sorry to lose you. Kind of you to come; but there was no real danger. You see, my dear little lady, all this talk about war saving, and secrecy, and keeping the blinds down at night, and so forth, is all very well; but unless it's carried out with intelligence, believe me, you may waste a pound to save a penny; you may let out all sorts of secrets to the enemy; you may guide the Zeppelins right on to your own chimneys. Thats where the ability of the governing class comes in. Shall the fellow call a taxi for you?

THE LADY   No, thanks: I prefer walking. Goodbye. Again, many, many thanks.

(She goes out. AUGUSTUS *returns to the writing-table smiling, and takes another look at himself in the mirror.* THE CLERK *returns with his head bandaged, carrying a poker)*

THE CLERK   What did you ring for? (AUGUSTUS *hastily drops the mirror*). Dont you come nigh me or I'll split your head with this poker, thick as it is.

AUGUSTUS   It does not seem to me an exceptionally thick poker. I rang for you to shew the lady out.

THE CLERK   She's gone. She run out like a rabbit. I ask myself, why was she in such a hurry?

THE LADY'S VOICE   (*From the street*) Lord Augustus. Lord Augustus.

THE CLERK   She's calling you.

AUGUSTUS   (*Running to the window and throwing it up*) What is it? Wont you come up?

THE LADY   Is the clerk there?

AUGUSTUS   Yes. Do you want him?

THE LADY   Yes.

AUGUSTUS   The lady wants you at the window.

THE CLERK   (*Rushing to the window and putting down the poker*) Yes, maam? Here I am, maam. What is it, maam?

THE LADY   I want you to witness that I got clean away into the street. I am coming up now.

(The two men stare at one another)

THE CLERK   Wants me to witness that she got clean away into the street!

123

George Bernard Shaw

AUGUSTUS   What on earth does she mean?

(THE LADY *returns*)

THE LADY   May I use your telephone?
AUGUSTUS   Certainly. Certainly. (*Taking the receiver down*) What
  number shall I get you?
THE LADY   The War Office, please.
AUGUSTUS   The War Office?
THE LADY   If you will be so good.
AUGUSTUS   But — Oh, very well. (*Into the receiver*) Hallo. This is
  the Town Hall Recruiting Office. Give me Colonel Bogey,
  sharp.

(*A pause*)

THE CLERK   (*Breaking the painful silence*) I dont think I'm awake.
  This is a dream of a movy picture, this is.
AUGUSTUS   (*His ear at the receiver*) Shut up, will you? (*Into the
  telephone*) What? . . .(*To* THE LADY) Whom do you want to
  get on to?
THE LADY   Blueloo.
AUGUSTUS   (*Into the telephone*) Put me through to Lord Hungerford
  Highcastle. . . . I'm his brother, idiot . . . That you, Blueloo?
  Lady here at Little Pifflington wants to speak to you. Hold
  the line. (*To* THE LADY) Now, madam (*He hands her the
  receiver*).
THE LADY   (*Sitting down in* AUGUSTUS'S *chair to speak into the
  telephone*) Is that Blueloo? . . . Do you recognize my voice?
  . . . Ive won our bet. . . .
AUGUSTUS   Your bet!
THE LADY   (*Into the telephone*) Yes: I have the list in my wallet. . . .
AUGUSTUS   Nothing of the kind, madam. I have it here in my
  pocket. (*He takes the envelope from his pocket; draws out
  the paper; and unfolds it*)
THE LADY   (*Continuing*) Yes: I got clean into the street with it. I have
  a witness. I could have got to London with it. Augustus wont
  deny it. . . .
AUGUSTUS   (*Contemplating the blank paper*) Theres nothing written
  on this. Where is the list of guns?

124

THE LADY   (*Continuing*) Oh, it was quite easy. I said I was my
sister-in-law and that I was a Hun. He lapped it up like a
kitten. . . .

AUGUSTUS   You dont mean to say that—

THE LADY   (*Continuing*) I got hold of the list for a moment and
changed it for a piece of paper out of his stationery rack: it
was quite easy (*She laughs; and it is clear that Blueloo is
laughing too*).

AUGUSTUS   What!

THE CLERK   (*Laughing slowly and laboriously, with intense enjoy-
ment*) Ha ha! Ha ha ha! Ha! (AUGUSTUS *rushes at him: he
snatches up the poker and stands on guard*). No you dont.

THE LADY   (*Still at the telephone, waving her disengaged hand
behind her impatiently at them to stop making a noise*)
Sh-sh-sh-sh-sh!! (AUGUSTUS, *with a shrug, goes up the
middle of the room.* THE LADY *resumes her conversation with
the telephone*) What? . . . Oh yes: I'm coming up by the
12.35: why not have tea with me at Rumpelmeister's . . .
Rum-pelmeister's. You know: they call it Robinson's now
. . . Right. Ta ta. (*She hangs up the receiver, and is passing
round the table on her way towards the door when she is
confronted by* AUGUSTUS)

AUGUSTUS   Madam: I consider your conduct most unpatriotic. You
make bets and abuse the confidence of the hardworked
officials who are doing their bit for their country whilst our
gallant fellows are perishing in the trenches—

THE LADY   Oh, the gallant fellows are not all in the trenches,
Augustus. Some of them have come home for a few days
hard-earned leave; and I am sure you wont grudge them a
little fun at your expense.

THE CLERK   Hear! hear!

AUGUSTUS   (*Amiably*) Ah, well! For my country's sake — !

After the Play Suggestions:

For Writing and Discussion

1. Satire is a type of writing that makes fun of people or institutions.
Why might this play be called a satire? What group is the target
of Shaw's play?

2. *Augustus Does His Bit* was written for soldiers during the first World War — the bloodiest war in history. Why should Shaw choose such a target (World War I) at that time? (You may need to do some research to answer this one.)

3. What is Augustus' attitude towards those he considers his inferiors? How do you imagine he came to think like this?

4. *Augustus Does His Bit* would very often have played to soldiers in the audience on leave from their units. Why would they be likely to enjoy this play?

5. Augustus says, "Our statesmen are the greatest known to history. Our generals are invincible. Our army is the admiration of the world." How might an audience of battle-weary soldiers react to these statements?

6. When Beamish asks for a "rise"(raise) in pay, Augustus tells him that everyone is making sacrifices and he should be making them too. Beamish tells him, "Not half, they aint. Wheres the baker's sacrifice? Wheres the coal merchant's? Wheres the butcher's? Charging me double: thats how they sacrifice themselves. Well I want to sacrifice myself that way too." Does Shaw put these words into Beamish's mouth just for comic effect or does he have a serious purpose? Explain.

7. You may have noticed that Shaw spells certain words in an unconventional way. Actually, he was a great student of language, and did this deliberately. What advantage do you think he might have seen in this way of spelling?

8. If you wanted to be sure that audiences understood the play's theme, how might you design the costumes of the actors?

9. Shaw describes this play as a "true-to-life farce." One aspect of farce is that the characters are often too exaggerated for an audience to believe that they could ever exist, yet Shaw calls it a true-to-life farce. What does he mean?

For Research and Further Reading

1. To understand something of what it felt like to be a soldier in those times, read some of the war poems of Wilfred Owen. Use your library as a source.

2. Shaw's play, *Pygmalion* (the idea behind *My Fair Lady*), tells you a great deal about his views on the English language. You might choose to read this play as well.

For Performance

1. Divide the class into four large groups, then divide each large group into smaller groups of two or three. With the help of your teacher, each smaller group should pick a short section of the play that is self-contained or "hangs together." Look at the section carefully and decide: (a) What is the most important thing that's going on? (b) What is each of the characters in the scene *trying to do?* For example, in the first couple of minutes of the play, you might decide that Augustus is trying to put Beamish in his place or, possibly, to find his *real* secretary. Whatever you decide, use this information to improvise the section of the play in your own words.

   When your improvisations are ready, each group should perform for the larger group of one-quarter of the class. While you perform your improvisation, the members of the large group will be playing the parts of the soldiers in the audience.

   Remember: Not all the soldiers will be privates, some will be officers; some will laugh at the play, while others will be angry. The eye needs *movement*. What possibilities can you find for action in an office?

127

$$\bigcirc\bigcirc\bigcirc\bigcirc\bigcirc\bigcirc\bigcirc$$

Schubert's Last Serenade

by Julie Bovasso

Note: *The language of this play has been altered for high school readers with permission of the copyright holder.*

Julie Bovasso is an actress, director and playwright who lives and works in New York City. In 1969 she was the recipient of a triple "Obie" award for acting, directing and writing for New York's Off-Broadway theatre club, La Mama. *Schubert's Last Serenade* was originally presented at La Mama in June 1971.

Before the Play

On paper, describe a situation from your past where you wanted to do a particular thing but, for reasons of your own, decided not to. Try to explain why you acted as you did. When you are finished, share your piece of writing with three or four members of the class.

Author's Note:

The action of the play occurs exactly as described by the MAÎTRE D'. *There are a few stage directions which are not spoken by him and which are indicated in the usual manner. The* MAÎTRE D' *stands outside the action of the play and should have no contact with the actors nor they with him.*

Characters:

THE MAÎTRE D'
ALFRED
BEBE
THE WAITER
THE COOK
FRANZ SCHUBERT

The houselights fade to black. A single spotlight picks up the MAÎTRE D' *standing at a lectern in a corner of the stage. He reads from a manuscript.*

MAÎTRE D'   An elegant French restaurant. In the darkness we hear Schubert's Serenade played on a violin. (*The music begins and the lights fade up very slowly on the scene*) Alfred, a young construction worker, dressed in overalls and hard-hat, is seated at a table with Bebe, a young Radcliffe sophomore with a badly bandaged head. They stare at each other with intense love. Behind a large potted palm, Franz

130

Schubert can be seen through the leaves, playing his violin. The waiter stands at his station, napkin folded over his arm, waiting.

(There is a long silence)

BEBE   I think it means something.
ALFRED   *(Nods)* Yeah.
BEBE   I mean, two people . . .
ALFRED   *(Nods)* Yeah, right.
MAÎTRE D'   The cook appears in the archway and shakes his fist fiercely at the palm tree. Franz Schubert stops playing and appears from behind the palm. The waiter looks from the cook to Franz Schubert. Franz Schubert looks from the waiter to the cook. The cook looks from Franz Schubert to the waiter; he makes another fierce gesture with his fist and exits angrily. The waiter follows him off quickly. Franz Schubert disappears behind the palm tree.

(FRANZ SCHUBERT plays again)

BEBE   I mean . . . it means something.
ALFRED   Yeah.
BEBE   Happenstance.
ALFRED   Yeah.
BEBE   Accident.
ALFRED   Yeah.
BEBE   Don't you think it means something?
ALFRED   Yeah.
MAÎTRE D'   Bebe brings her hand slowly up from her lap and moves it along the table toward Alfred. Alfred then brings his hand slowly up from his lap and moves it along the table toward Bebe. As their hands meet and touch they knock over a large glass vase. The music stops abruptly. Alfred and Bebe rise in confusion and embarrassment. Franz Schubert appears from behind the palm tree and glares at them. The waiter appears with a dustpan and brush and cleans up the mess. He glares at Alfred and Bebe, and exits. Franz Schubert disappears behind the palm tree, and Alfred and Bebe resume their original positions and try to recapture their love spell. There

is a long silence. Franz Schubert plays again. Alfred and Bebe recapture their love spell and sit staring at each other with intense passion.

BEBE   Twice in two weeks.

ALFRED   Twice, right.

BEBE   It can't be an accident.

ALFRED   No.

BEBE   It has to mean something.

ALFRED   Right.

BEBE   It has to mean *something*.

ALFRED   Yeah.

MAÎTRE D'   The cook pokes his head through the archway again and shakes his fist at the palm tree. The music stops abruptly. Suddenly, Bebe turns to the cook and shakes her fist fiercely at him. He rushes off. Alfred wipes his brow nervously with the napkin.

ALFRED   Wow! Some goings on.

MAÎTRE D'   Franz Schubert plays again. There is another long pause while Alfred and Bebe get back into their love spell.

BEBE   I mean, why us?

MAÎTRE D'   Alfred nods. But he does not make eye contact.

BEBE   It's such a large city, millions of people . . . why us?

MAÎTRE D'   Pause.

BEBE   And twice. *Twice* in two weeks.

ALFRED   Right, twice.

BEBE   It's no accident.

ALFRED   No.

BEBE   It was planned.

ALFRED   Right.

BEBE   By some higher power.

ALFRED   Right.

BEBE   It was planned by some higher power that we should meet.

MAÎTRE D'   Bebe listens to the serenade, wistfully carried off by the romance of the moment. Alfred is uncomfortable and sits with his head down, glancing around with lowered eyes.

BEBE   I mean, you and me . . . from opposite ends of the stratum.

MAÎTRE D'   Alfred looks up, startled.

BEBE   Opposite ends of the stick.

ALFRED   Oh.

BEBE   In a city with millions of people . . .

ALFRED   Yeah.

BEBE   We stumble, we fall. Twice.

ALFRED   Right. We stumble, we fall.

BEBE   Twice.

ALFRED   Right.

MAÎTRE D'   The waiter appears with two glasses of red wine. He places them on the table and, with a hostile glance at Alfred, exits. Alfred shifts uncomfortably in his seat. Bebe picks up her glass in a toast. Alfred does likewise.

BEBE   You know, the first time we stumbled across each other, I fell.

ALFRED   Oh, yeah?

BEBE   Down there in front of the Customs Building. Did you fall for me the first time we stumbled across each other?

ALFRED   Yeah.

BEBE   I knew it.

ALFRED   I didn't mean to crack your skull.

BEBE   Oh, but it was meant to be. I mean, why *my* head? Why not some other head? Don't you see? Don't you understand?

ALFRED   Yeah. I think so.

BEBE   *Your* club found its way to *my* head. I mean . . . *mine*!

ALFRED   That's true. It was your head. Not some other head.

BEBE   Not just *any* head. Don't you think that's magical?

ALFRED   Yeah.

MAÎTRE D'   Franz Schubert stops playing and appears from behind the palm tree. He stands looking at them with an expression of unbelievable disgust.

BEBE   And just before I blacked out and fell, I knew that I had fallen.

ALFRED   For me.

BEBE   Yes. Just before I fell, I knew that I was falling . . . for you. Oh, I mean I was falling for The Cause, but while I was falling for The Cause, I simultaneously fell for you. It was a double fall, you might say. The moment you raised your club, I started to fall. I fell even before you struck. But if you hadn't struck, I wouldn't have fallen.

ALFRED   For me.

BEBE   No, for The Cause.

ALFRED   Would you have fallen for me if you hadn't fallen for The Cause? I mean, anyway?

MAÎTRE D'   Bebe frowns suddenly and, with a nervous little gesture, brings her hand to her chin.

BEBE   (*Evasively*) Have you got a cigarette?

ALFRED   (*Insistently*) Would you?

BEBE   I really would like a cigarette.

ALFRED   Answer my question?

BEBE   What question? (THE COOK *and* THE WAITER *appear*)

ALFRED   If I hadn't cracked your skull with my club and given you cause to fall for your Cause, would you have fallen for me anyway?

BEBE I don't understand the question.

MAÎTRE D' She starts to rise. Alfred grabs her roughly by the arm.

ALFRED Would you have fallen for me if you hadn't fallen for The Cause?

BEBE You're hurting my arm!

ALFRED Is it me or The Cause, baby?

BEBE You're making a scene.

ALFRED Let's have it straight or I'll break your skull!

MAÎTRE D' Bebe emits a cry of ecstasy and falls into his arms in a swoon. The waiter, the cook and Franz Schubert look from one to the other. Alfred holds Bebe's limp body, not knowing quite what to do with it. Finally, he puts her back into her chair. The cook and the waiter exit with hostile glances at Alfred. Franz Schubert disappears behind the palm tree. Alfred sits stiffly in his chair. Bebe finally opens her eyes.

ALFRED Well?

BEBE I haven't been quite honest with you.

ALFRED That's what I thought.

BEBE If you hadn't struck me that first time and given me the opportunity to fall for The Cause, I might not have fallen for you at all.

MAÎTRE D' Alfred rises angrily . . .

ALFRED That's what I thought!

MAÎTRE D' . . . Flings his napkin on the table, picks up his tool box and starts to leave.

BEBE Alfred, wait! (*She rises and grabs his arm.* ALFRED *stops, stands with his back to her*) Don't leave me like this. Give me a chance to explain. It's all very complex. Please don't destroy something precious. It was the second time that I was really hooked, and whether or not the first time had happened, the second time would have happened anyway.

MAÎTRE D' Franz Schubert has come out from behind the palm tree and stands listening with interest.

BEBE Don't you see? Whether or not I knew consciously that first time whether I had fallen for you because you'd made me fall for The Cause or whether I'd have fallen for you anyway doesn't matter. It was the second time, on the Ganesvort Street pier.

MAÎTRE D' Franz Schubert is confused.

BEBE That second time was the time I knew that this time it was for real. (THE WAITER *has entered with* THE COOK) When I saw you marching on that line in front of the pier, carrying that picket sign which read "Save the Pier," and I arrived carrying a sign which read exactly the same thing! Oh, Alfred! That was the moment. It was the moment I realized that *we were on the same side!*

MAÎTRE D'   She pauses and waits for some reaction. None is forthcoming. Desperately, she turns to Franz Schubert, the cook and the waiter for help.

BEBE   Don't you see? I realized that we were on the same side! (*Turning back to* ALFRED) You, who had cracked my skull viciously two weeks earlier and sent me reeling to the ground for my Cause!

MAÎTRE D'   Alfred does not respond. She turns to Franz Schubert, the cook and the waiter again and attempts feverishly to explain.

BEBE   (*To* FRANZ SCHUBERT) Don't you see? All my mixed emotions suddenly came together. All the confusion of love and hate jelled.

MAÎTRE D'   Franz Schubert looks at the waiter.

BEBE   (*To the* WAITER) Love jelled into hate . . .

MAÎTRE D'   The waiter looks at the cook.

BEBE   (*To the* COOK) Hate jelled into love . . .

MAÎTRE D'   The cook looks at Franz Schubert.

BEBE   And suddenly I understood everything!

MAÎTRE D'   They all look at each other in total confusion.

BEBE   *I understood my feelings about that first time at the Customs House!*

MAÎTRE D'   Bebe turns desperately to Alfred, who is still not listening.

BEBE   I understood why I had felt that gnawing guilt about loving you, Alfred!

MAÎTRE D'   At the mention of his name, Alfred turns.

BEBE   And because of that guilt, I had denied the truth to myself. I understood why I wanted to fling myself into your arms the moment you raised your club. I understood why I wanted to wrap myself around you and kiss you madly on the eyes in front of the world while the clubs were swinging and the rocks were flying and the bricks were hurtling through the air!

MAÎTRE D'   The cook and the waiter leave. Franz Schubert straightens his tie self-consciously and goes behind the palm tree.

ALFRED   Are you saying that you would have fallen for me anyway? Even if I hadn't clubbed you?

BEBE   Yes!

ALFRED   Okay.

135

MAÎTRE D′ They return to the table and resume their love spell with even greater intensity. Franz Schubert plays again, slightly off key.

(The music plays for awhile, before BEBE *speaks)*

BEBE You know, Alfred, life is funny.

ALFRED Yeah.

BEBE I might not have known it if the second time hadn't happened.

MAÎTRE D′ Alfred is immediately suspicious.

ALFRED *(Suspiciously)* Waddayamean?

BEBE I mean the Ganesvort Street pier. When I saw that we were on the same side it substantiated all the irrational emotions which I experienced at the Customs House.

ALFRED Oh, right.

BEBE You were fighting to save the pier. I was fighting to save the pier . . .

ALFRED It's the union. The union is behind it all. The union is behind everything.

BEBE The union is behind its men.

ALFRED The men are behind the union.

MAÎTRE D′ Franz Schubert appears from behind the palm tree with a savage look on his face.

BEBE The union is behind our love!

MAÎTRE D′ Franz Schubert flings his violin violently across the room. Alfred and Bebe rise in confusion. Franz, in a state of utter agitation, is feverishly mopping his face with a handkerchief. He then crosses the room and picks up his violin. The waiter enters hurriedly and tries to calm Franz Schubert, patting his head and brushing off his coat. Then, with an angry glare at Alfred and Bebe, he takes Franz behind the palm tree. Alfred and Bebe return to their chairs and sit stiffly. The waiter approaches them.

WAITER *(Coldly)* Would you like to order now, please? The cook is getting impatient.

ALFRED Oh, yeah. Sure. We'll order now. Fine.

BEBE No! We'll wait!

MAÎTRE D′ The waiter glares at her with fury, turns abruptly and exits.

ALFRED You shouldn't have done that. He's really mad. Maybe he needs the table.

BEBE   Posh. We're not here to accommodate him; he's here to accommodate us.

ALFRED   That's true. I never thought of it that way.

MAÎTRE D'   Franz Schubert comes out from behind the palm tree. He has completely recovered his composure and his manner is very disdainful and haughty. He moves to a table upstage and sits, crossing his legs and looking smugly at Alfred and Bebe. They glance at him; he smirks back at them and turns away with a derisive grin. He then raises his hand and summons the waiter.

ALFRED   (*Leaning across the table and whispering*) He's mad, too. I don't think he's going to play anymore.

MAÎTRE D'   The waiter enters with a glass of wine for Franz Schubert. Franz raises the glass in mock toast to Alfred and Bebe. The waiter laughs. Then Franz Schubert laughs with the waiter.

ALFRED   I'll rap 'em *both* in the head!

BEBE   Don't pay attention to them. They're trying to arouse us. If we ignore them they'll stop.

MAÎTRE D'   Alfred glares angrily at Franz Schubert and the waiter, who smirk back at him. The waiter then leans over to Franz and whispers something in his ear. Franz nods. The waiter laughs. Then they both laugh and glance at Alfred and Bebe.

ALFRED   I'll break that violin over his fat head!

MAÎTRE D'   Alfred rises.

BEBE   No, Alfred, no! Sit down. I hate violence.

ALFRED   (*Advancing on* FRANZ SCHUBERT *and the* WAITER) Did you hear me? I'll break that violin over your fat head!

MAÎTRE D'   Franz Schubert scurries behind the palm tree and the waiter rushes off into the kitchen. Alfred stands in the centre of the room with his fists clenched and bellows loudly.

ALFRED   Let's have a little service around this dump!

BEBE   Alfred, please! You're making a scene. Sit down.

ALFRED   What is this crap around here? Who the hell runs this joint? What kind of help have you got in this freak house restaurant? (FRANZ SCHUBERT, *the* WAITER *and the* COOK *appear*)

BEBE   Alfred, please. Come and sit down. We were talking about us, Alfred, remember? Us. Look at me, Alfred. Love. It's the only solution.

MAÎTRE D'   Alfred rises suddenly and slams his fist on the table.

ALFRED   You! Bring us some menus!

MAÎTRE D'   The waiter rushes off. Alfred turns to Franz Schubert.

ALFRED   You! Go play your violin!

MAÎTRE D'   Franz Schubert disappears behind the palm tree and plays frantically, at a much faster tempo. Alfred turns to the cook.

ALFRED   You! Get back into your kitchen, quick!

MAÎTRE D'   The cook hobbles off. Alfred sits. Bebe stares at him with admiration.

BEBE   You're marvellous.

ALFRED   (Modestly) It was nothing.

BEBE   No, it was something. It really was something. I mean . . .

ALFRED   It was nothing. Nothing.

BEBE   . . . To be aroused to such passion, such fury, such . . .

ALFRED   It was nothing.

BEBE   Just like that! Without any cause.

MAÎTRE D'   Alfred is immediately on his guard.

ALFRED   Waddayamean?

BEBE   I mean, I envy you. I really do. I mean, I wish I could be aroused without any cause.

ALFRED   Waddayamean, without any cause? I had a cause. They caused it.

BEBE   Well, small cause to warrant such a big reaction.

ALFRED   Oh, yeah?

BEBE   You overreacted.

ALFRED   Oh, yeah?

BEBE   And I suspect it's because you don't have a larger cause to react to.

MAÎTRE D'   She leans over and touches his hands gently.

BEBE   Poor Alfred. If only you could harness your fury to an ideal.

ALFRED   (Pulling his hands away) Getattaheah.

BEBE   What's the matter? You're suddenly angry with me.

ALFRED   Yeah, I'm angry. I'm angry as hell! First you say I'm marvellous and then you take it all back.

BEBE   I didn't take it all back. I simply adjusted my initial reaction.

ALFRED   You adjusted it all right.

MAÎTRE D'   He rises angrily . . .

ALFRED   You threw a wet rag on the whole thing!

MAÎTRE D'   . . . Flings his napkin on the table . . .

ALFRED   I've had it!

MAÎTRE D'   . . . And starts to leave.

ALFRED   I'm going home!

BEBE   No, Alfred, please! Don't leave like this. Why can't we discuss things without getting angry and walking out? You're so compulsive, so irrational. You don't leave any room for differences. If you don't like something you get up and walk out. That's running away, Alfred, running away from infinite possibilities.

ALFRED   Yeah? Well, I'm still going home.

BEBE   I want to understand you, Alfred. I want to know you. And I want you to understand me and know me. What good is love without understanding? How can we love each other if we don't know each other and understand each other? How can we understand each other if we don't know each other? And how can we know each other if we don't love each other?

ALFRED   Okay.

MAÎTRE D'   Alfred returns to the table, somewhat sullenly. There is a long silence. Bebe observes him clinically.

BEBE   (Patronizingly) Why did you come back?

ALFRED   What?

BEBE   Why did you come back?

ALFRED   (Angrily) I came back because I came back.

BEBE   (Persisting) But why? Why did you come back? Do you know why? Have you thought about it?

ALFRED   No, I haven't thought about it. I haven't had time to think about it.

BEBE   There you go, getting angry again. Why are you angry? What did I say to make you angry? (She begins to cry) I can't open my mouth without you shouting at me. Every word I say, you shout at me . . . like a bully.

MAÎTRE D'   The cook enters disguised as a lady flower-seller.

ALFRED   Do you want a flower? Don't cry. I'll buy you a flower. Hey, you! (The COOK crosses to their table) Which one do you want?

BEBE   That one. (She takes the flower and ALFRED gives the COOK a dollar. The COOK leaves. BEBE sits sniffing it for a moment) it doesn't smell. It's fake.

MAÎTRE D'   She flings the flower on the table. Alfred picks it up and sniffs it.

ALFRED   You're right. It's fake.

MAÎTRE D'   He rises quickly and begins to bellow again.

ALFRED   Fake! She sold us a fake flower! Where did she go? Hey! Flower-seller! Come back here, you fake! We don't want your fake flowers, understand?

MAÎTRE D'   Franz Schubert and the waiter appear.

BEBE   Alfred, sit down. It doesn't matter.

ALFRED   Waddayamean, it doesn't matter? (To FRANZ SCHUBERT and the WAITER) Where's that flower-seller? She sold me a fake flower!

BEBE   Alfred, sit down, please. You're making a scene. It's nothing.

ALFRED   Waddayamean, it's nothing! It's a fake! When I buy something real I don't want it to be fake.

BEBE   It doesn't mean that much. It's only a flower.

ALFRED   It's not a flower, it's a fake! A flower is a flower and a fake is a fake and I can't stand anything that's fake.

BEBE   This is embarrassing. Alfred, I don't care about the flower. It doesn't mean that much to me. Please, sit down.

MAÎTRE D'   Alfred finally calms down and sits. Franz Schubert disappears behind the palm tree; the waiter starts to leave but decides not to.

BEBE   You see what I mean? You get so violent and passionate over such small things.

ALFRED   It's not a small thing.

BEBE   It's only a flower.

ALFRED   It isn't a flower!

BEBE   It isn't the end of the world.

ALFRED   It's the idea behind it!

BEBE   There is no idea behind it. You feel cheated, that's all.

ALFRED   All! All! Damned right I feel cheated! And that's not all! I feel so damned cheated over that damned fake paper flower . . .

MAÎTRE D'   He picks up the flower and rips it to shreds . . . and flings it into the air.

ALFRED   I hate anything that's fake!

MAÎTRE D'   Exhausted, he sits down, his head in his hands. Bebe strokes his back gently.

BEBE   I understand. Poor Alfred. You get so passionate over nothing.

ALFRED   That's why I clubbed you. Because you gimme that fake smile. Fake!

BEBE   (*Startled*) What?

ALFRED   Yeah, yeah, fake. Waddaya think, I'm blind? I seen the expression on your face when I raised my club down there at the Customs House. You were ready to kill. You were ready to tear me apart, and I thought, Wow! This chick is outa sight. This chick is gonna beat the living hell outa me! But no! Waddaya do? You cop-out, that's what. Pppftt! Just like that. Sudden. You go soft on me and you smile. You gimme that little Jesus-Christ-on-the-cross smile, and in a second I know that you want *me* to club *you*. You expect me to club you. So I club you! Otherwise you wouldn'ta gimme that fake smile. You woulda tore into me the way you really wanted to. You'da scratched my face and bit my flesh and

I'd of thought, Wow! This is a real chick! But no. Waddaya do? You stop. You stop just long enough to . . . adjust your initial reaction and you fake-out! Fake! Fake! Fake! Somebody should've split your skull long ago, let you know where it's at!

BEBE   You really are a beast, aren't you? An animal. And you're a coward on top of it all. Oh, big strong man with a steel hat and a club, coming at a lot of defenceless women and students . . .

ALFRED   Fakes! Fakes! And I hate anything that's fake. You're no woman. You're a *fake*. Fake-out! Fake!

BEBE   Oh, how could I have deluded myself into thinking I loved you? You are the lowest, the most primitive, the most despicable . . .

ALFRED   Right! But I'm *real*. I'm not fake!

BEBE   You're everything I've always loathed. How can I have imagined that I loved you? ! How is it possible? How can I have even conceived the idea? Oh, Daddy! Daddy! All these years I've despised you, Daddy, because you were a gentleman, a man of refinement, a man of sensibilities, a man of education. Quiet, understanding, always willing to sit down and discuss a problem. Oh, Daddy, Daddy. I've betrayed you. Daddy. Betrayed you with this *beast*!

MAÎTRE D'   The waiter approaches the table.

WAITER   Excuse me, sir. I'll have to ask you to remove your hat.

ALFRED   Remove my hat?

WAITER   Yes. We don't permit gentlemen in the dining room with their hats on.

ALFRED   I'm sorry, but I'm not removing my hat.

WAITER   You'll have to leave unless you remove your hat.

ALFRED   I'm not removing my hat and I'm not leaving!

BEBE   (*Screaming*) Oh, God! Oh, God! You're making a scene. Take off the hat!

ALFRED   Shaddap!

BEBE   My father would take off *his* hat!

ALFRED   I'm not your father!

BEBE   Oh, God!

WAITER   Why won't you take off your hat?

ALFRED   Because it's my hat!

WAITER   (*To* BEBE) Why won't he take off his hat?

BEBE   Because it's a symbol. Not a hat. If he takes it off he'll have an identity crisis.

WAITER   I see. (*He exits*)

MAÎTRE D'   Bebe rises and begins to collect her things.

141

ALFRED   What are you doing?

BEBE   I'm leaving, that's what I'm doing.

ALFRED   Leaving?

MAÎTRE D'   Alfred rises and grabs her arm.

ALFRED   Waddayamean, leaving?

BEBE   It's over. Let go of my arm!

ALFRED   Waddayamean, over? Where do you think you're going?

BEBE   Home. It's all over. Finished. I don't love . . . love you. It was a mistake.

ALFRED   Waddayamean, a mistake?

BEBE   Let me go!

MAÎTRE D'   Bebe pulls away and rushes toward the exit.

ALFRED   What's a mistake? Come back here!

MAÎTRE D'   Alfred grabs her again. She struggles.

BEBE   Let me go. It was all an illusion. A mistake.

ALFRED   Well, which was it, an illusion or a mistake?

BEBE   Let me go, you brute!

MAÎTRE D'   Alfred cracks her across the jaw. (ALFRED *does not follow this direction. Repeating*) Alfred cracks her across the jaw. (ALFRED *still does not follow the direction. He holds* BEBE'S *arms*)

ALFRED   You can't go. I dig you.

MAÎTRE D'   Bebe screams and rushes off. (BEBE *does not follow this direction. They both remain fixed, looking at each other. The* MAÎTRE D' *repeats the direction very firmly*) Alfred cracks her across the jaw. Bebe screams and rushes off.

BEBE   (*Softly*) You called me a fake.

ALFRED   So what? So you're a fake. I dig you.

MAÎTRE D'   (*Shouting*) *Alfred cracks her across the jaw.* BEBE *screams and rushes off.*

BEBE   You said you hate fakes.

ALFRED   I do. But I still dig you.

MAÎTRE D'   (*Commanding like a Nazi*) *Alfred cracks her across the jaw . . . !*

ALFRED   . . . And something is telling me that I oughta crack you across the jaw but I don't want to.

MAÎTRE D'   *Bebe screams and rushes off!*

ALFRED   Because I dig you.

MAÎTRE D'   *Bebe screams and rushes off!*

BEBE   (*Softly*) I dig you, too.

MAÎTRE D'   *Bebe screams and rushes off, do you hear what I am saying?* (*The* WAITER *returns, alarmed*)

BEBE   . . . And something is telling me that I should leave, but I don't want to. It's as though something has *always* been telling me to do one thing when I've wanted to do something else. It's been that way all my life . . . as though I've been following some invisible stage directions.

MAÎTRE D'   (*Desperately*) *Alfred cracks her across the jaw!* (ALFRED *kisses* BEBE *tenderly*) *Bebe screams and rushes off!*

WAITER   Franz Schubert appears from behind the palm tree, smiling. (FRANZ SCHUBERT *appears, smiling*)

MAÎTRE D'   (*Whirling on the* WAITER) You're fired!

FRANZ SCHUBERT   (*Raising his bow*) Franz Schubert raises his bow and begins to play, magnificently. (*He plays*)

MAÎTRE D'   You're *all* fired!

COOK   (*Entering with tray*) The cook appears with a tray of coconut milk.

MAÎTRE D'   What coconut milk? I will have no coconut milk!

WAITER   The Maître D' flings his script across the room, kicks over the lectern and charges off like an angry savage.

MAÎTRE D'   (*As he does so*) You're all fired! Through! Finished! Do you hear? You're finished, Schubert! D'ya hear me?! Finished! And you! And you! And you! And you! (*He disappears*)

WAITER   (*Taking the tray from the* COOK *and serving*) The waiter hands a coconut to Alfred, to Bebe, and to the cook, and they all drink their coconut milk while Franz Schubert plays, magnificently. (*The music swells and the lights fade on all drinking coconut milk*)

Curtain

After the Play Suggestions:

For Writing and Discussion

1. The central characters in this play, Bebe and Alfred, don't seem very realistic. Would they be more believable without the maître d' reading the stage directions? Why or why not?

2. (a) On formal occasions, such as going to an expensive restaurant or a wedding, we often seem to feel and act differently. Why?

   (b) In what way are formal occasions like being in a play?

143

3. Why does Alfred's behaviour in the restaurant make Bebe so upset?
4. Is the maître d' a character in this play or is he outside it? Explain.
5. Near the end of the play, Bebe comments, "And something is telling me that I should leave but I don't want to. It's as though something has *always* been telling me to do one thing when I've wanted to do something else. It's been that way all my life. . . . as though I've been following some invisible stage directions."
   (a) It might be said of this play that the maître d' is a sort of playwright telling the characters what they should feel and do. By the end of the play they have all rebelled against him. Why?
   (b) Can actors and actresses rebel against a playwright? Explain.

6. We are not characters in a play, but most of us have our own internal "stage directions" (things that tell us what we should or should not do).
   (a) Where do you think these "stage directions" come from?
   (b) Is it possible to act differently from our "stage directions"? Explain your answer.

For Performance

In groups of four or five, carefully read the play out loud. When you have done so, decide the direction in which the maître d' is trying to push Bebe and Alfred (and the others). Imagine that there is a second maître d' who wants them all to do something entirely different. Try improvising the play with the two maître d's struggling for control of the other characters. When you get the scene to work well, decide which of the maître d's wins and why. When you feel confident, perform your improvisation for another group or for the class.